EMBEDDED
formative
asse

DYLAN WILIAM

555 North Morton Street
Bloomington, IN 47404
800.733.6786 (toll free) / 812.336.7700
FAX: 812.336.7790

email: info@solution-tree.com
solution-tree.com

Solution Tree
Jeffrey C. Jones, CEO & President

Solution Tree Press
President: Douglas M. Rife
Publisher: Robert D. Clouse
Vice President of Production: Gretchen Knapp
Managing Production Editor: Caroline Wise
Senior Production Editor: Lesley Bolton
Proofreader: Elisabeth Abrams
Text and Cover Designer: Jenn Taylor

For Siobhán Leahy

Acknowledgments

This book is the result of a thirty-five year journey that has taken me from public school teacher to teacher educator to researcher and university administrator. Given the length of this journey, you will not be surprised that I have a lot of people to thank. First, the students at Christopher Wren School and North Westminster Community School in London taught me most of what I know about learning. The research I have read and carried out since then has done little more than help me make sense of what I learned there. Second are the teachers I have worked with in those two schools and in the extended networks of teachers of which I have been a part. As someone who went straight from a bachelor's degree to the classroom, with no training or preparation, I was fortunate to start teaching in one of London's toughest schools—fortunate because every teacher in that school struggled and was willing to talk about their struggles. It is only subsequently that I have realised how lucky I was, because that openness is not found everywhere.

Mentioning individuals is always invidious, but I owe particular debts of gratitude to Sarah Sharkey and Jerry Hardy (Christopher Wren School) and Dick Gmiterek (North Westminster Community School). When I joined the University of London, I lucked out again, being mentored by two great thinkers about education—first, Margaret Brown and later, Paul Black. As well as being extraordinary academics, they are two of the nicest people one could ever hope to meet, and their generosity to younger academics is a model I have tried to emulate. I am also grateful to the editorial staff at Solution Tree, and particularly Lesley Bolton, for all the work they have done in getting my manuscript to the finished book you have before you. Finally, and most importantly, my greatest thanks go to my partner, Siobhán Leahy. We first met at a mathematics teachers' conference over thirty years ago, and for thirty years, she has been my greatest inspiration, my greatest support and has kept me grounded in the realities of daily school life. That is why the book is dedicated to her.

Table of Contents

About the Author

Dylan Wiliam, PhD, is a consultant who works with educators in North America, the United Kingdom, and many other countries to develop effective, research-based formative assessment practices. He is former deputy director of the Institute of Education at the University of London. From teaching in urban public schools to directing a large-scale testing program to serving in university administration, his professional path has led to a variety of positions at the forefront of education. Dr Wiliam was also, from 2003 to 2006, senior research director at the Educational Testing Service in Princeton, New Jersey.

During his early years of teaching in inner-city classrooms, Dr Wiliam focused on physics and mathematics. He later joined the faculty of Chelsea College, University of London, which later became part of King's College London. Here, he worked on developing innovative assessment schemes in mathematics before accepting leadership of the King's College Mathematics Education Program.

For three years, Dr Wiliam served as the academic coordinator of the Consortium for Assessment and Testing in Schools, which developed a variety of assessments for the national curriculum of England and Wales. He then returned to King's College to serve as dean of the School of Education before being promoted to assistant principal of the college.

In 1998, he coauthored a major review of research evidence on formative assessment with Paul Black and has worked with many teachers in the United Kingdom and United States on developing formative assessment practices to support learning.

In addition to a doctor of education, Dr Wiliam holds numerous degrees in mathematics and mathematics education. To learn more about Dr Wiliam's work, visit www.dylanwiliam.net.

To book Dr Wiliam for professional development, contact pd@solution -tree.com.

Introduction

In 1984, I left my job teaching maths and science in an urban public school in London to join a research project at the University of London that was exploring the potential of formative assessment to improve student learning. Over a quarter of a century later, this book is the result of that journey.

The book has two main purposes. The first is to provide simple, practical ideas about changes that every teacher can make in the classroom to develop his or her practice of teaching. The second is to provide the evidence that these changes will result in improved outcomes for learners.

In chapter 1, I show why educational achievement is so important and why raising educational achievement needs to be a national priority; with higher levels of educational achievement, people are healthier, live longer, contribute more to society and earn more money. For society, the benefits include reduced criminal justice costs, reduced health care costs and increased economic growth.

I also outline briefly how previous attempts at reform—including changes to the structure of schooling, to the governance of schools, and to the curriculum, and an increased role for digital technology—have been largely ineffective. These reform efforts have failed to take into account three crucial points:

1. The quality of teachers is the single most important factor in the education system.

2. Teacher quality is highly variable.

3. Teacher quality has a greater impact on some students than others.

In chapter 1, I also show that attempts at improving the quality of entrants into teaching and removing the least effective teachers will result in small effects that will take a generation to materialise. The fundamental argument of chapter 1, therefore, is that to secure our future economic prosperity, we need to help the teachers who are already serving in our schools improve.

In chapter 2, I explore some of the ways that teachers might develop and estimate how big an impact these changes would have on student outcomes. I show that some popular initiatives, such as learning styles, have no discernible impact on student achievement at all, while others, such as increasing teacher content knowledge, do improve student learning but by much less than is generally assumed.

In the second part of chapter 2, I summarise the research on classroom formative assessment practices and show that these practices appear to have a much greater impact on educational achievement than most other reforms. Chapter 2 concludes by outlining what formative assessment is, and what it is not, and presents the five key strategies of formative assessment.

Chapters 3, 4, 5, 6 and 7 deal in turn with each of the five key strategies of formative assessment:

1. Clarifying, sharing and understanding learning intentions and criteria for success

2. Engineering effective classroom discussions, activities and learning tasks that elicit evidence of learning

3. Providing feedback that moves learning forward

4. Activating learners as instructional resources for one another

5. Activating learners as owners of their own learning

In each of these five chapters, I present a summary of the research evidence that shows the impact of the strategy, and I offer a number of practical techniques that teachers have used to incorporate the strategy into their regular classroom practice. Although there is a definite progression throughout the chapters, I have made each chapter as self-contained as possible.

In all, these five chapters describe over fifty practical techniques for classroom formative assessment. Most of these techniques are not new; what is new is the framework for formative assessment that is presented in chapter 2, which shows how these disparate techniques fit together, and the research evidence that shows that these are powerful ways of increasing student engagement and helping teachers make their teaching more responsive to their students' needs.

CHAPTER 1

Why Educational Achievement Matters

Educational achievement matters—more now than at any time in the past. It matters for individuals, and it matters for society. For individuals, higher levels of education mean higher earnings, better health and increased life span. For society, higher levels of education mean lower health care costs, lower criminal justice costs and increased economic growth. In this chapter, we will explore why education is vital to the prosperity of every nation and why the vast majority of attempts by policymakers to improve the achievement of school students has failed.

The Increasing Importance of Educational Achievement

Education has always been important, but it has never been as important as it is now. Figure 1.1 (page 4) shows how the average hourly rate of pay (in 2007 dollars) of American workers has changed since the 1970s, depending on the level of educational achievement (Economic Policy Institute, 2010).

Figure 1.1 shows that in 1973, the average secondary school dropout could expect to earn around $13 per hour. By 2005, however, a secondary school dropout could expect to earn less than $11 per hour. This is really rather extraordinary. On average, people living in the United

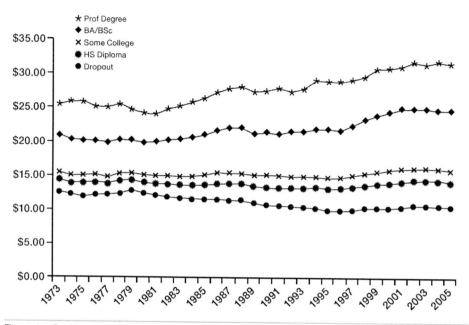

Figure 1.1: Real hourly wages (in 2007 dollars) 1973–2005 by level of education.

States today are much better off in real terms than they would have been in 1973. But if you are a secondary school dropout, you are worse off than you would have been in 1973. The biggest gainers have been those with advanced degrees. In 1973, they earned on average approximately twice as much as secondary school dropouts. By 2005, it was almost three times as much.

Higher levels of education are also associated with better health; people with more education are less susceptible to a whole range of diseases, including cancer, and are less likely to have a significant period of disability toward the end of their lives (Jagger, Matthews, Melzer, Matthews, Brayne & MRC Cognitive Function and Ageing Study, 2007). No doubt this is partly due to lifestyle choices, such as smoking, but it is also due in part to the kinds of work that are available to those with limited education. Only 75 per cent of adult Americans who did not complete secondary school report being in good health, while the figure for those with a bachelor's degree is 95 per cent (Organisation for Economic Co-operation and Development, 2010).

People with more education live longer. Between 1915 and 1939, at least thirty US states changed their child labour laws and periods of compulsory schooling. As a result, a number of students were required to attend school for one more year than others. By looking at the life spans of those who had been required to attend an extra year of school, Adriana Lleras-Muney (2005) estimated that one additional year of school adds 1.7 years to one's life. These are high stakes indeed.

Educational achievement also matters for society. Henry Levin and his colleagues at Columbia University have estimated that preventing one secondary school dropout produces a net benefit to society of $209,000 (Levin, Belfield, Muennig, & Rouse, 2007). The main components of this total are:

- $139,000 in extra taxes the individual would pay because he or she would be earning more money

- $40,500 in reduced health care costs, partly because the individual would be healthier, as noted previously, but also partly because he or she would be more likely to get health benefits from an employer and, therefore, be less dependent on public assistance

- $26,600 in reduced criminal justice costs (largely because the individual would be less likely to be incarcerated)

Higher levels of education are needed in the workplace. It is common to hear employers complaining about a "skills shortage", claiming that young people entering the workforce today are less skilled than those in the past. In fact, on a whole range of measures, young people today are substantially more skilled than their parents and grandparents.

Scores on standardised tests, such as the Wechsler intelligence tests, have been rising steadily. Only one in six students who took the Wechsler test in 1947 scored as high as the average student in 2001 did. Table 1.1 (page 6) shows how much higher the average student of 2001 scored than the average student of 1947, in percentiles (based on Flynn, 2007).

Some of these gains are truly extraordinary. Only 6 per cent of children in 1947 performed as well as the *average* child of 2001 on the Similarities test. No-one is entirely sure what has caused these remarkable increases (Neisser, 1998), but there is little doubt that these gains in capabilities are real—and meaningful. So if today's children are more skilled than their parents and grandparents, why are employers so unhappy? Perhaps it's the teachers.

However, the quality of teaching in public schools is, on average, higher than in private schools in the United States, as is shown

Table 1.1: Score Gains on the Wechsler Intelligence Scale for Children, 1947 to 2001

WISC subtest	Percentile increase from 1947 to 2001
Information	6
Arithmetic	6
Vocabulary	12
Comprehension	27
Picture completion	28
Block design	36
Object assembly	38
Coding	38
Picture arrangement	42
Similarities	44

by data collected by the Organisation for Economic Co-operation and Development (OECD) as part of their Programme for International Student Assessment (PISA, 2007). Every three years since 2000, nationally representative samples of fifteen-year-olds from over forty countries have participated in tests of reading literacy, mathematical literacy and scientific literacy. Unlike the tests developed for other international comparisons, such as those used by the Trends in International Mathematics and Science Study (TIMSS), the PISA tests have been specifically designed to assess the ability of students to apply their knowledge rather than just reproduce it. Since students are selected at random to participate in these tests, and they are low-stakes tests for both teachers and students, it seems unlikely that students in either private schools or public schools will have been coached for these tests, so the scores should be a reasonable indication of the level of skills possessed by American fifteen-year-olds.

As might be expected, the scores of students attending private schools in the United States were higher than those attending public schools. In 2006, students attending public schools averaged 485 in science and 470 in maths. The figures for private schools were 554 and 534, respectively. (The gap is approximately the same as that between the top-performing country, Finland, and the average of all participating countries.)

This, however, does not show that private schools are better than public schools, because the students who go to private schools are not the same as those who go to public schools. Not only do students from more affluent backgrounds score better, but their presence in schools also raises the achievement of the students around them, sometimes called "peer effects". To control for this, the PISA survey collected information about the economic, social and cultural status of the students. When the scores were controlled for the social background of the students and of the schools, the score advantage for the private schools disappeared; private and public schools performed similarly (PISA, 2007). However, the average class size was nineteen in the private schools and twenty-six in the public schools. All other things being equal, the OECD data show that private school teachers achieve with classes of nineteen what public school teachers achieve with classes of twenty-six, which is strong evidence that the quality of instruction in public schools is higher than that in private schools.

So if students are smarter and teaching is better, why are so many employers dissatisfied with the educational achievement of our public schools? The answer lies in the changing nature of the world of work. Schools have improved dramatically, but the changes in the workplace have been even more extraordinary.

In the 1960s and '70s, the average workingman (or woman) needed neither to read nor to write during the course of a workday; there were many jobs available to those with limited numeracy and literacy skills, but now those jobs are disappearing. Extrapolating from studies done in other countries (for example, Patel, Kelly, Amadeo, Gracey & Meyer, 2009), it is likely that the United States economy is shedding 2500 low-skill jobs every day. Some are being outsourced to countries with lower labour costs, but far more are being destroyed by technology. In the 1960s, it was common to find fifty or more people working on milling machines and lathes in an engineering workshop. Now, the same work is done—and with a greater degree of accuracy—by one person managing fifty computer numerically controlled (CNC) machines. The United States is still a leading manufacturer—still making things, but using far fewer people to do so.

We are, in fact, entering a completely new era. Up until now, productive employment has been available to almost all adults of working age. Whether this will continue to be the case is by no means certain. It is as if we are walking up a down escalator. In the past, the rate at which our schools generated skills was greater than the rate at which low-skill jobs were being destroyed, so we made progress. But the speed of the down escalator has been increasing—technology and outsourcing are removing jobs from the economy—and if we cannot increase the rate at which our schools are improving, then, quite simply, we will go backward. Higher levels of educational achievement lead to increased economic growth, and every developed nation is in a race. But this race is not primarily against other countries. It is a race with technology.

Changes in technology actually affect white-collar jobs more than they affect blue-collar jobs. As David Autor and his colleagues (Autor, Levy & Murnane, 2003) have shown, certain kinds of white-collar jobs have been disappearing faster than blue-collar jobs (see table 1.2). For example, if you went to a savings and loan in the 1970s to ask for a mortgage, a human being would have made the decision; now it's done by a computer, using data such as your credit score.

Table 1.2: Change in Workplace Skill Demand in the United States: 1969–1999

Skill category	Change
Complex communication	+14%
Expert thinking and problem solving	+8%
Routine manual	-2%
Non-routine manual	-5%
Routine cognitive	-8%

While many of these routine cognitive jobs have been automated, others have been offshored, and the trend for offshoring is likely to accelerate. Alan Blinder (2010), an economist at Princeton University, showed that at least one-fourth of the jobs existing in the United States in 2004 were probably "offshorable". Most people assume that low-skill jobs are those primarily at risk, but in fact, Blinder shows that the correlation between skill and offshorability is close to, if not actually, zero. Routine data entry work and jobs as call-centre operators were among the first to be outsourced, but now high-skilled jobs are outsourced, too. If you need an X-ray examined at 3 a.m., the image might be sent to radiologists in India (Burute & Jankharia, 2009), which is probably good news because they are likely to be both highly skilled and awake! Developments in robotic telesurgery mean that advanced surgical techniques such as those for prostate surgery and brain surgery are likely, in the near future, to be performed by surgeons thousands of kilometres away from the patient, so even the most advanced forms of surgery are now offshorable. Skill is no longer an antidote to the problem of offshoring.

If having a valued skill no longer guarantees employment, then the only way to be sure of being employable is to be able to develop new skills, as Seymour Papert (1998) observed:

> So the model that says learn while you're at school, while you're young, the skills that you will apply during your lifetime is no longer tenable. The skills that you can learn when you're at school will not be applicable. They will be obsolete by the time you get into the workplace and need them, except for one skill. The one really competitive skill is the skill of being able to learn. It is the skill of being able not to give the right answer to questions about what you were taught in school, but to make the right response to situations that are outside the scope of what you were taught in school. We need to produce people who know how to act when they're faced with situations for which they were not specifically prepared.

This is why education—as opposed to training—is so important. Not only does education confer skills, but it also produces the ability to develop new skills.

The fundamental idea that education is the engine of future economic prosperity has been understood for many years, but recent work has shown just how much education increases economic growth (or conversely, just how much economic growth is limited by low educational achievement).

In a report for the OECD, Eric Hanushek and Ludger Woessmann attempted to estimate the economic value of increases in student achievement (Hanushek & Woessmann, 2010). As their measure of educational achievement, they used a variety of tests of reading, mathematics and science achievement, including those that the OECD had developed for PISA. Hanushek and Woessmann examined the likely economic impact of a twenty-five-point increase in scores on PISA over a twenty-year period—this is actually less than the improvement achieved by the most rapidly improving country, Poland, in just six years, between 2000 and 2006. They calculated that the net value of such an improvement to the United States would be over $40 trillion—approximately three times the US national debt. Getting every student's achievement up to 400 (the OECD's definition of minimal proficiency) would be worth $70 trillion, and matching the performance of the world's highest-performing countries (such as Finland) would be worth over $100 trillion.

Why Is Raising Student Achievement So Hard?

Successive governments have understood the importance of educational achievement and have sought to raise standards through a bewildering number of policy initiatives. Although most of these seemed like sensible measures at the time, the depressing reality is that the net effect of the vast majority of these measures on student achievement has been close to, if not actually, zero.

A number of reform efforts have focused on the *structures* of schooling. In the United States, particular attention was given to reducing school size. The logic was simple: many secondary schools are very large and impersonal, and so the creation of smaller secondary schools should produce more inclusive learning communities, which should then result in better learning. However, the promise of such smaller secondary schools was not always realised. In many cases, large secondary schools of around 3000 students were divided into five or six smaller secondary schools, each with 500 or 600 students but housed in the same building. Often, in such cases, the only change was to increase administrative costs, as a result of appointing six new principals for each of the small secondary schools and increasing the compensation of the existing principal for looking after six newly appointed junior principals.

In other cases, the potential benefits of small secondary schools were not realised because the creation of small secondary schools was assumed to be an end in itself, rather than a change in structure that would make other needed reforms easier to achieve. One benefit claimed was that smaller secondary schools would improve staff-student relationships, and with improved relationships, students would become more engaged in their learning. Students would interact with a smaller number of teachers, thus fostering the development of better staff-student relationships. This may well be effective, although it has to be said that getting students engaged so that they can be taught something seems much less efficient than getting them engaged *by* teaching them something that engages them. But every student would still have an English teacher, a maths teacher, a science teacher, a geography teacher and so on. The number of teachers a student meets in a day is not affected by the size of the secondary school. The development of staff-student relationships *is* strengthened if teachers loop through with their students (so that the same teacher teaches a class for more than a single semester or year), but this requires amendments to schedules and also depends on having teachers who are able to teach multiple year levels. This could easily be done in large secondary schools, if it were felt to be a priority.

Other countries are going in the opposite direction. In England, for example, principals of high-performing schools are being asked to assume responsibility for less successful schools by forming "federations" of schools, but as yet, there is no evidence that this has led to improvement.

Other reforms have involved changes to the governance of schools. The most widespread such reform in the United States has been the introduction of charter schools. Forty states and the District of Columbia have charter laws (Hill, Angel, & Christensen, 2006), but the evaluations of their impact on student achievement do not allow any easy conclusions to be drawn. There is no doubt that some charter schools are achieving notable success, but others are not, and there appear to be more of the latter than the former. According to a report from the Center for Research on Education Outcomes (CREDO) at Stanford University, approximately one-half of charter schools get similar results to traditional public schools, one-third get worse results, and one-sixth get better results (CREDO, 2009). The net effect of the introduction of charter schools, therefore, appears to be a slight *lowering* of student achievement, although this may be due to the fact that most charters actually get less money per student (Miron & Urschel, 2010). It is important to note also that the effects of charter schools, even when they are successful, appear to be small on average. An evaluation of the charter school system in Chicago (Hoxby & Rockoff, 2004) did find that students attending charter schools scored higher on the Iowa Tests of Basic Skills, but the effects were small: an increase of 4 percentile points for reading and just 2 percentile points for maths. As the characteristics of successful charter schools become better understood, it will, no doubt,

be possible to ensure that charter schools are more successful, but at the moment, the creation of charter schools cannot be guaranteed to increase student achievement (Carnoy, Jacobsen, Mishel, & Rothstein, 2005).

In England, a number of low-performing schools have been reconstituted as "academies" that are run by philanthropic bodies but receive public funds equivalent to public schools, in addition to a large capital grant for school rebuilding. The principals of these academies have far greater freedom to hire and fire staff and are not required to follow national agreements on teacher compensation and benefits, nor are they required to follow the national curriculum. Student test scores in these academies have risen faster than those in regular public schools, but this is to be expected, since such schools start from a lower baseline. A comparison with similarly low-performing schools that were *not* reconstituted as academies shows that they improve at the same rate (Machin & Wilson, 2009).

One of the most radical experiments in the organisation of schooling has been taking place in Sweden. In the early 1990s, for-profit providers were invited to run public schools. Although a number of evaluations of this initiative found some successes, each of these studies contained significant methodological weaknesses. A more recent evaluation, which corrected the flaws of earlier studies, found that the introduction of for-profit education providers did produce moderate improvements in short-term outcomes such as year nine GPA and in the proportion of students who chose an academic secondary school track. However, these improvements appeared to be concentrated in more affluent students and were transient. There was no impact on longer-term outcomes such as secondary school GPA, university attainment or years of schooling (Böhlmark & Lindahl, 2008).

In England, since 1986, secondary schools have been allowed to apply for "specialist school" status. Specialist schools do get higher test scores than traditional secondary schools in England, but they also get more money—around $200 more per student per year. The improvement in results achieved by specialist schools turns out to be just what you would expect if you just gave the public schools an extra $200 per student per year (Mangan, Pugh & Gray, 2007). Moreover, specialist schools do not get better results in the subjects in which they specialise than they do in other subjects (Smithers & Robinson, 2009).

Other reform efforts have focused on curriculum. Almost every country aspires to have a "curriculum for the 21st century". For instance, the Scottish government has adopted a "Curriculum for Excellence", but whether anything changes in Scottish classrooms remains to be seen, because, as we have learned from decades of curriculum reform, changes in curriculum rarely impact practice in classrooms. Trying to change students' classroom experience through changes in curriculum is very difficult. A bad curriculum well taught is invariably a better experience for students than a good curriculum badly taught: pedagogy trumps curriculum. Or more precisely, pedagogy *is* curriculum, because what matters is how things are taught, rather than what is taught.

There are different levels of curriculum. There is the intended curriculum: what policymakers adopted. There is the implemented curriculum: what actually got incorporated into textbooks and other classroom materials. And then there is the achieved curriculum: what actually happened when teachers used those textbooks and materials in classrooms. The greatest impact on learning is the daily lived experiences of students in classrooms, and that is determined much more by *how* teachers teach than by *what* they teach.

Textbooks play an important role in mediating between the intended and the achieved curriculum, and as a result, there has been great interest in finding out whether some textbook programs are more effective than others. Reviews of random-allocation trials of programs for reading in the early years and for programs in primary, middle years and secondary school maths concluded that there was little evidence that changes in textbooks alone had much impact on student achievement. It was only when the programs changed teaching practices and student interactions that a significant impact on achievement was found (Slavin & Lake, 2008; Slavin, Lake, Chambers, Cheung & Davis, 2009; Slavin, Lake & Groff, 2009).

Many reforms look promising at the pilot stage but, when rolled out at scale, fail to achieve the same effects. In 1998, after less than a year in office, Tony Blair's Labour government launched the National Literacy Strategy and, a year later, the National Numeracy Strategy for primary schools in England and Wales. Although these programs showed promising results in the early stages, their effectiveness when rolled out to all primary schools was equivalent to one extra eleven-year-old in each primary school reaching proficiency per year (Machin & McNally, 2009). Bizarrely, the fastest improvement in the achievement of English eleven-year-olds was in science, which had not been subject to any government reform efforts.

Other reform efforts have emphasised the potential impact of educational technology, such as computers, on classrooms. While there is no shortage of boosters for the potential of computers to transform education, reliable evidence of their impact on student achievement is rather harder to find. The history of computers in education is perhaps best summed up by the title of a book by Stanford professor Larry Cuban (2002): *Oversold and Underused*.

This is not to say that computers have no place in education. Some computer programs are extremely effective at teaching difficult content matter. One of the best examples is the Cognitive Tutor: Algebra I, developed over a period of twenty years at Carnegie Mellon University (Ritter, Anderson, Keodinger & Corbett, 2007). The program has a very specific focus—teaching procedural aspects of year-nine algebra—and is therefore intended only to be used for two or three hours per week, but the evidence suggests that the program is better at teaching this than all but the best 5 per cent of algebra teachers (Ritter et al., 2007). However, such examples are rare, and computers have failed to revolutionise our classrooms in the way predicted. As Heinz Wolff once said, "The future is further away than you think" (Wolff & Jackson, 1983).

More recently, attention has focused on the potential of the interactive whiteboard. In the hands of expert practitioners, these are stunning pieces of educational technology, but as a tool for improving educational outcomes at scale, they appear to be very limited. We know this from an experiment that took place in London. The English secretary for education, Charles Clarke, was so taken with the interactive whiteboard that he established a fund that doubled the number of interactive whiteboards in London schools. The net impact on student achievement was zero (Moss et al., 2007). But, say the technology boosters, you have to provide professional development to go with the technology. This may be so, but if interactive whiteboards can only be used effectively when teachers are given a certain number of hours of professional development, then surely it is right to ask whether the same number of hours of professional development could be more usefully, and less expensively, used in another way.

As a final example of an effort to produce substantial improvement in student achievement at scale, it is instructive to consider the impact of teachers' aides in England. One large-scale evaluation of the impact of support staff on student achievement found that teachers' aides actually lowered the performance of the students they were assigned to help (Blatchford et al., 2009). Of course, this does not mean that the use of teachers' aides cannot increase student achievement—merely that they have not.

The reform efforts discussed here, and the history of a host of other reform efforts, show that improving education at scale is clearly more difficult than is often imagined. Why have we pursued such ineffective policies for so long? Much of the answer lies in the fact that we have been looking in the wrong place for answers.

Three Generations of School Effectiveness Research

Economists have known about the importance of education for economic growth for years, and this knowledge has led to surges of interest in studies of "school effectiveness".

Some schools appeared to get consistently good test results, while others seemed to get consistently poor results. The main thrust of the first generation of school effectiveness research, which began in the 1970s, was to understand the characteristics of the most effective schools. Perhaps if we understood that, we could reproduce the same effect in other schools. Unfortunately, things are rarely that simple. Trying to emulate the characteristics of today's most effective schools would lead to the following measures:

1. First, get rid of the boys. All over the developed world, girls are outperforming boys, even in traditionally male-dominated subjects such as maths and science. The more girls you have in your school, the better you are going to look.

2. Second, become a parochial school. Again, all over the world, parochial schools tend to get better results than other schools, although this appears to be more due to the fact that parochial schools tend to be more socially selective than public schools.

3. Third, and most important, move your school into a nice, leafy, suburban area. This will produce three immediate benefits.

First, it will bring you much higher-achieving students. Second, the students will be better supported by their parents, whether this is in terms of supporting the school and its mission or paying for private tuition even though the student is not making the progress desired. Third, the school will have more money—potentially lots more. Some schools receive more than $25,000 per student per year, whereas others receive less than $5000 per student per year.

In case it wasn't obvious, these are not, of course, serious suggestions. Girls' schools, parochial schools and schools in affluent areas get better test scores primarily because of who goes there, rather than how good the school is, as was pointed out in the second generation of school effectiveness studies. These researchers pointed out that most of the differences between school scores are due to the differences in students attending those schools rather than any differences in the quality of the schools themselves. The OECD PISA data are helpful in quantifying this.

The PISA data show that 74 per cent of the variation in the achievement of fifteen-year-olds in the United States is within schools, which means that 26 per cent of the variation in student achievement is between schools. However, around two-thirds of the between-school variation is caused by differences in the students attending that school. This, in turn, means that only 8 per cent of the variability in student achievement is attributable to the school, so that 92 per cent of the variability in achievement is not attributable to the school. What this means in practice is that if fifteen out of a class of thirty students achieve proficiency in an average school, then seventeen out of thirty would do so in a "good" school (one standard deviation above the mean) and thirteen out of thirty would do so in a "bad" school (one standard deviation below the mean). While these differences are no doubt important to the four students in the middle who are affected, they are, in my experience, much smaller than people imagine. It, therefore, seems that Basil Bernstein (1970) was right when he said that "education cannot compensate for society" and that we should be realistic about what schools can, and cannot, do (Thrupp, 1999).

However, as better quality data sets have become available, we have been able—in the third generation of school effectiveness studies—to dig a little deeper and focus on what contributes to the school's "value added" (the difference between what a student knew when he arrived at a school and what he knew when he left). It turns out that as long as you go to school (and that's important), then it doesn't matter very much which school you go to, but it matters very much which classrooms you're in.

In the United States, the classroom effect appears to be at least four times the size of the school effect (PISA, 2007), which, predictably, has generated a lot of interest in what might be causing these differences. It turns out that these substantial differences between how much students learn in different classes have little to do with class size, how the teacher groups the students for instruction or even the presence of between-class grouping practices (for example, tracking). The most critical difference is simply the quality of the teacher.

Parents have always understood how important having a good teacher is to their children's progress, but only recently have we been able to quantify exactly how much of a difference teacher quality makes.

The Impact of Teacher Quality

For many years, it seems, most people involved in education assumed that the correlation between teacher quality and student progress was effectively zero. In other words, as long as they were properly qualified, all teachers were equally good, so on average, students should progress at the same rate in all classrooms. Of course, different students would progress at different rates according to their talents and aptitudes, but the assumption was that all teachers were pretty comparable and therefore were treated like a *commodity*.

To an economist, a commodity is a good for which there is a demand, and it is *fungible*—one unit can be substituted for another, since all are assumed to be of equal quality. It is convenient for policymakers to treat teachers as a commodity, because then teacher compensation can be determined on a supply-and-demand basis. Teacher compensation could—like that for traders on the financial markets—be set on the basis of the value they contribute, but this would mean that the best teachers would cost way too much—over $300,000 per year according to one study (Chetty et al., 2010). Politicians prefer to set a standard for "the qualified teacher", and everyone who meets that standard gets in. Teacher compensation is then determined by supply and demand—how much needs to be paid to get a qualified teacher in every classroom (although in this context, it is worth noting that this is not the basis that politicians tend to use to determine their own pay!).

The desire of teacher unions to treat all teachers as equally good is understandable, because it generates solidarity among their members, but more importantly because performance-related pay is *in principle* impossible to determine fairly. Consider a region that tests its students every year from year three to year eight and then uses the test score data to work out which teachers have added the most value each year. This looks straightforward, but there is a fatal flaw: no test can capture all that is important for future progress. A year-four teacher who spends a great deal of time developing skills of independent and collaborative learning, who ensures that her students become adept at solving problems, and who develops her students' abilities at speaking, listening and writing in addition to teaching reading may find that her students' scores on the year-four maths and reading tests are not as high as those of other teachers in her school who have been emphasising only what is on the test. And yet, the teacher who inherits this class in year five will look very good when the results of the year-five tests are in, not because of what the year-five teacher has done, but because of the firm foundations that were laid by the year-four teacher.

In addition, evidence suggests that paying teachers bonuses for the achievement of their students does not raise test scores. Between 2006 and 2009, teachers in Nashville, Tennessee, were selected at random and offered bonuses of $15,000 for getting their students' achievement to match the highest-performing 5 per cent of students, with lesser bonuses of $10,000 and $5000 for matching the highest-performing 10 per cent and 20 per cent, respectively. An evaluation of the incentives found that the scores of the students taught by teachers who were offered the bonuses were no higher than those taught by other teachers (Springer et al., 2010).

Many economists are surprised by such results. They assume that people are motivated primarily by economic rewards and so offering cash incentives for people to try harder must surely increase results. They forget that such incentives work only when people are not already trying as hard as they can. There are, no doubt, some teachers who do not care about how well their students do, and for this small minority of teachers, incentives may work. But the vast majority of teachers are trying everything they can to increase their students' achievement. There is certainly no evidence that there are teachers who are holding onto a secret proven method for teaching fractions until someone pays them more money. So performance-related pay is impossible to implement fairly, does not seem to work, and even if it can be made to work, will make a difference only for that small minority of teachers who are not already trying their best.

As noted previously, for many years, it was assumed that one teacher was as good as another, providing each was adequately qualified for the job. However, in 1996, William Sanders and June Rivers published a paper based on an analysis of 3 million records on the achievement of Tennessee's entire student population from year two to year eight. The important feature of this database was that it allowed Sanders and Rivers to identify which students had been taught by which teachers in which year level. They found that there were differences in how much students learned with different teachers and that these differences were large. To show how large the differences were, they classified the teachers into five equally sized groups based on how much progress their students had made (low, below average, average, above average and high). They then examined how an average eight-year-old student would fare, depending on what teachers he or she got. What they found was rather surprising. A student who started year two at the 50th percentile of achievement would end up at the 90th percentile of achievement after three years with a high-performing teacher but, if assigned to the classes of low-performing teachers for three years, would end up at the 37th percentile of achievement—a difference of over 50 percentile points. They found that increases in teacher quality were most beneficial for lower-achieving students, and the general effects were the same for students from different ethnic backgrounds (Sanders & Rivers, 1996).

More recent studies (for example, Rockoff, 2004; Rivkin, Hanushek & Kain, 2005) have confirmed the link between teacher quality and student progress on standardised tests, and it appears that the correlation between teacher quality and student progress is at least 0.2, and may be even larger (Nye, Konstantopoulos & Hedges, 2004). One way to think about this is that an increase of one standard deviation in teacher quality increases student achievement by 0.2 standard deviation, which is equivalent to an increase in achievement of around 6 percentile points for average students.

Another way of thinking about the effects of teacher quality is in terms of the rate of learning. Take a group of fifty teachers. Students who are fortunate enough to be taught by the most effective teacher in that group will learn in six months what those taught by the average teachers will take a year to learn. And those taught by the least effective teacher in that group of fifty teachers are likely to take two years to learn the same material. In other words, the most effective teachers generate learning in their students at four times the rate of the least effective teachers.

Just as important, teacher quality appears to play a significant role in promoting equality of outcomes. In the United States, many policymakers seem to have assumed that excellence and equity are somehow in tension—that we can have one or the other, but not both. However, evidence from international comparisons has shown that the countries with the high average scores also tend to have a narrow range of achievement (Bursten, 1992). The relationship between the mean scores of year four students in mathematics in the thirty-six countries participating in the 2007 TIMSS study and the spread of scores in each country (measured in standard deviations) is shown in figure 1.2. It is clear that there is a strong trend for the countries with the highest average achievement

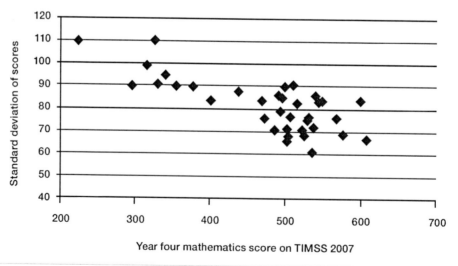

Figure 1.2: Relationship between mean and spread of year four maths scores.

to have much closer outcomes for their young people (the correlation between means and standard deviations is in fact -0.75).

As noted previously, Sanders and Rivers (1996) found that increases in teacher quality conferred greater benefits on low achievers than high achievers, and a particularly well-designed study of fifteen- and sixteen-year-olds (Slater, Davies & Burgess, 2008) also found that the benefits of having a high-performing teacher were greatest for low achievers (although interestingly, they also found that high achievers benefited more than those of average achievement). In their work in kindergarten and year one classrooms, Bridget Hamre and Robert Pianta (2005) found that in the classrooms of the teachers whose students made the most progress in reading, students from disadvantaged backgrounds made as much progress as those from advantaged backgrounds, and those with behavioural difficulties progressed as well as those without.

This last finding is particularly important because it shows that Basil Bernstein was wrong—education *can* compensate for society *provided it is of high quality*. Ideally, in the short term, we would concentrate on how to get the highest-quality teachers to the students who need them most. Currently, the evidence is that teacher quality is reasonably randomly distributed in the United States. There *are* systematic differences in the levels of teacher certification and teacher compensation between the most affluent and least affluent areas, but as we have seen, these have little impact on teacher quality. Because the lowest achievers need high-quality teachers, the random allocation of teachers will not produce equitable outcomes. Equitable outcomes will only be secured by ensuring that the lowest-achieving students get the best teachers, which, in the short term, means taking them away from the high-achieving students; this is politically challenging to say the least.

In the longer term, a focus on improving teacher quality will mean that teacher allocation will no longer be a zero-sum game. At the moment, our focus on the achievement gap draws attention to the gap between the high achievers and the low achievers. The problem with thinking about this as an issue of "gaps" is that one can reduce the gap either by improving the performance of the lowest achievers *or by reducing the achievement of the highest achievers*. This leads back to the traditional, and now discredited, thinking that equity is the enemy of excellence. Rather than thinking about narrowing the gap, we should set a goal of proficiency for all, excellence for many, with all student groups fairly represented in the excellent. And the way to achieve this is simply to increase teacher quality. As Michael Barber says, "the quality of an education system cannot exceed the quality of its teachers" (Barber & Mourshed, 2007, p. 19).

How Do We Increase Teacher Quality?

The realisation that teacher quality is the single most important variable in an education system has led to an exploration of how teacher quality can be improved, and there are really only two options. The first is to attempt to replace existing teachers with better ones, which includes both deselecting serving teachers and improving the quality of entrants to the profession. The second is to improve the quality of teachers already in the profession.

Because past attempts to improve the performance of serving teachers have achieved so little success, a number of authors suggest that the only way to improve the profession is through replacement, including both rigorous deselection (Hanushek, 2010) and increasing the threshold for entry into the profession.

Teacher deselection may be politically attractive—after all, who could possibly be against getting rid of ineffective teachers? But it is hard to do, it may not work anyway, and even when it does work, it is a slow process. It is hard to do because, although we know that teachers make a difference, it is very difficult, if not impossible, to work out who really are the least effective teachers. It may not work because, to be effective, you have to be able to replace the teachers you deselect with better ones, and that depends on whether there are better potential teachers not currently teaching. Jack Welch famously believes in getting rid of the lowest-performing 10 per cent of employees each year (Welch & Welch, 2005). Such an approach sounds a little like the joke that "firings will continue until morale improves", but even if it does not have a negative impact on those who are not fired, it is only effective if one can replace the deselected 10 per cent with better employees. When those recruited to fill the vacancies are worse than those fired, the 10 per cent rule is guaranteed to *lower* average employee quality.

The third problem with deselection is that it is very slow. Replacing the lowest 10 per cent with teachers who are only slightly better will take many years to have any noticeable impact on average teacher quality. Given the difficulty with deselecting the right teachers, it is natural that much attention has focused instead on improving the quality of entrants into the profession.

Just increasing the quality of those aspiring to be teachers won't be enough, though, because at the moment, we have little idea how to select the best. This doesn't matter in countries like Finland, where teaching is held in such high esteem that the competition for places in teacher preparation courses is intense and only the highest-achieving third of all university students can get in (Ingersoll, 2007). They have so many talented people wanting to be teachers that they can afford to reject people who would actually be very good teachers. They only consider those with the highest university marks and then screen out those who don't have the communication skills and those who want to be teachers only because they like their subject—after all, to be a good teacher, you have to like working with children and young people; you're going to spend quite a long time with them over the coming years. The result is that in Finland, a lot of people who could be good teachers get rejected—that's tough on them, but at a system level, it doesn't matter very much because the country gets as many good teachers as it needs. However, countries like Australia can't afford to be so profligate. We can't afford to turn away anyone who might be a good teacher, so we need to have better ways of identifying in advance who will be good teachers, and it turns out to be surprisingly difficult, because many of the things that people assume make a good teacher don't.

Many people assume that university marks predict how good a teacher will be, and certainly one would expect that a measure of the knowledge that teachers need to teach well would somehow be associated with how much students learn, but the studies that have been done have found little or (more often) no correlation between teacher qualifications and student progress. It has been well known for quite a while that teachers' university marks have no consistent relationship with how much their students will learn, and some have gone so far as to claim that the only teacher variable that consistently predicts how much students will learn is teacher IQ (Hanushek & Rivkin, 2006). This suggests that it is the general intellectual calibre of teachers, rather than what they learn in college, that matters most.

Some progress has been made in determining what kinds of teacher knowledge do contribute to student progress. For example, scores achieved by primary school teachers on a test of mathematical knowledge for teaching (MKT) developed by Deborah Ball and her colleagues at the University of Michigan did correlate significantly with their students' progress in mathematics (Hill, Rowan & Ball, 2005). Although the effect was greater than the impact of socioeconomic status or race, it was in real terms small; a one standard deviation increase in a teacher's mathematical knowledge for teaching was associated with a 4 per cent increase in a student's rate of learning. In other words, students taught by a teacher with good MKT (that is, one standard deviation above the mean) would learn in fifty weeks what a student taught by an average teacher would learn in fifty-two weeks—a difference, but not a big one. Or, to put it another way, we saw earlier that one standard deviation of teacher quality increases the rate of student learning by around 50 per cent, and we have just seen that one standard deviation of pedagogical content knowledge increases the rate of student learning by 4 per cent. This suggests that subject knowledge accounts for less than 10 per cent of the variability in teacher quality.

A study of over 13,000 teachers, involving almost 1 million items of data on over 300,000 students in the Los Angeles Unified School District (LAUSD), found that student progress was unrelated to their teachers' scores on licensure examinations, nor were teachers with advanced degrees more effective (Buddin & Zamarro, 2009). Most surprisingly, there was no relationship between the scores achieved by LAUSD teachers on the Reading Instruction Competence Assessment (which all primary school teachers are required to pass) and their students' scores in reading. As the researchers themselves note, since this test is a requirement for all primary school teachers, those who fail the test are not permitted to teach, and so we cannot conclude that the test is not effective in screening out weaker teachers, but the results do suggest that the relationship between teachers' knowledge of reading pedagogy and student progress in reading is, at best, weak and perhaps nonexistent.

In an article in the *New Yorker*, Malcolm Gladwell (2008a) likens this situation to the difficulties of finding a good quarterback for the

National Football League (NFL). Apparently, for most positions, how well a player plays in university predicts how well he will fare in the NFL, but at quarterback, how well a player plays in university seems to be useless at predicting how well he will play in the pros.

One theory about why good—and often even outstanding—university quarterbacks failed in the NFL was that the professional game was so complex (Gladwell, 2008a). So now, all prospective quarterbacks take the Wonderlic Personnel Test—a fifty-item test that assesses arithmetic, geometric, logical and verbal reasoning. Unfortunately, as a number of studies have shown (for example, Mirabile, 2005), there does not appear to be any clear relationship between scores on the Wonderlic and how good a quarterback will be in the NFL. In 1999, for example, of the five quarterbacks taken in the first round of the draft, only one—Donovan McNabb—is likely to end up in the Hall of Fame, and yet his score was the lowest of the five. Other quarterbacks scoring in the same range as McNabb include Dan Marino and Terry Bradshaw—widely agreed to be two of the greatest quarterbacks ever.

Although efforts continue to try to predict who will do well and who will not within the NFL, Gladwell suggests that there is increasing acceptance that the only way to find out whether someone will do well in the NFL is to try him out in the NFL.

The same appears to be true for teaching. It may be that the only way to find out whether someone has what it takes to be a teacher is to try her out in the classroom, even though Thomas Kane and Douglas Staiger have estimated that we might need to try out four prospective teachers to get one good one (Gladwell, 2008a, p. 41) and that looks prohibitively expensive.

Even if we could identify in advance who would make the best teachers, doing anything useful with that information would take a long time. Suppose, for example, we could predict exactly how good each teacher was going to be. Suppose also that we had the luxury of so many people wanting to be teachers that we could raise the bar to a level whereby only two-thirds of those who are currently entering the profession would get in. Such a change would take thirty years to work through. The new, improved teachers would, in the first year, be only 3 per cent of the teaching force, 6 per cent in the second year, and so on. Not until all the teachers who had started teaching before we raised the bar had actually retired would the full effect be felt. And the effect, in thirty years' time, would be to increase teacher quality by around one-half of a standard deviation. If we assume that the correlation between teacher quality and student progress is 0.2, then the effect of this improvement in teacher quality would be to increase student achievement by 0.1 standard deviation, or 4 percentile points. The result? One extra student passing a standardised test every three years.

We can't wait that long. While deselecting the least effective teachers and trying to raise the quality of those entering the profession will have some effects, they are likely to be small and nothing like the kinds of improvements in teacher quality we need. If we are serious about securing our economic future, we have to help improve the quality of those teachers already working in our schools—what Marnie Thompson, my former colleague at ETS, calls the "love the one you're with" strategy.

Conclusion

Improving educational outcomes is a vital economic necessity, and the only way that this can be achieved is by increasing the quality of the teaching force. Identifying the least effective teachers and deselecting them has a role to play, as does trying to increase the quality of those entering the profession, but as the data and the research studies examined in this chapter have shown, the effects of these measures will be small and will take a long time to materialise. In short, if we rely on these measures to raise student achievement, the benefits will be too small and will arrive too late to maintain our status as one of the world's leading economies. Our future economic prosperity, therefore, depends on investing in those teachers already working in our schools.

CHAPTER 2

The Case for Formative Assessment

We've discussed how increasing the educational achievement of students is a national economic priority, and the only way to do that is to improve teacher quality. We also saw that deselecting existing teachers and improving the quality of entrants into the profession will have, at best, marginal effects, and so securing our economic future boils down to helping teachers who are already in post become more effective.

This chapter reviews the research on teacher professional development and shows that while there are many possible ways in which we could seek to develop the practice of serving teachers, attention to minute-by-minute and day-to-day formative assessment is likely to have the biggest impact on student outcomes. The chapter concludes by defining what, exactly, formative assessment is.

Professional Development

Andrew Leigh (2010) analysed a data set that included test scores on 90,000 Australian primary school students and found that, as in the American research, whether the teacher had a master's degree made no difference. He did, however, find a statistically significant relationship between how much a student learned and the experience of the teacher, as can be seen in figure 2.1 (page 28).

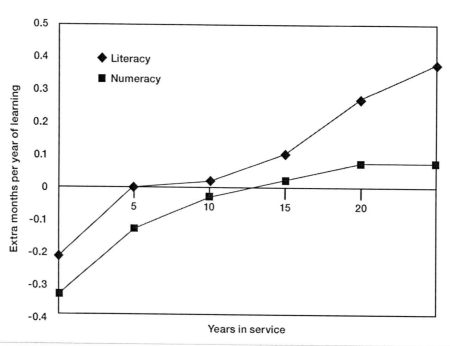

Figure 2.1: Increases in teacher productivity with experience (Leigh, 2010).

It is clear that the value added by a teacher increases particularly quickly in the first five years of teaching, but what is most sobering about figure 2.1 is the vertical axis. If a student is taught literacy by a twenty-year veteran, the student will learn more than he will if taught by a novice, but not much more. In a year, with a twenty-year veteran, a student will make an extra half-month's progress—in other words, a twenty-year veteran teacher achieves in fifty weeks what a novice teacher will take fifty-two weeks to achieve. Because of the size of the study, this result is statistically significant, and the improvement is worth having, but it is not a large difference. Therefore, it's not surprising that many have argued that the answer is more, and better, professional development for teachers.

Indeed, it would be hard to find anyone who would say that teacher professional development is unnecessary. Professional development for serving teachers is a statutory requirement in many jurisdictions. However, most of these requirements are so loosely worded as to be almost meaningless. Pennsylvania's Act 48 requires teachers to undergo 180 hours of professional development that is related to an educator's certificate type or area of assignment. Note that there is no requirement for teachers to improve their practice or even to learn anything. The only requirement is to endure 180 hours of professional development.

Many schools justify these requirements with the need for teachers to keep up to date with the latest developments in the field, but such a justification merely encourages teachers to chase the latest fad. One year, it's language across the curriculum; the next year, it's differentiated instruction. Because teachers are bombarded with innovations, none of these innovations has time to take root, so nothing really changes. And worse, not only is there little or no real improvement in what happens in classrooms, but teachers get justifiably cynical about the constant barrage of innovations to which they are subjected. The reason that teachers need professional development has nothing to do with professional updating. As far as I am aware, there haven't been any real breakthroughs in teaching for the last two thousand years. Teachers need professional development because the job of teaching is so difficult, so complex, that one lifetime is not enough to master it.

The fact that teaching is so complex is what makes it such a great job. At one time, André Previn was the highest-paid film-score composer in Hollywood, and yet one day, he walked into his office and quit. People asked him why he had given up this amazing job, and he replied, "I wasn't scared anymore." Every day, he was going in to his office knowing that his job held no challenges for him. This is not something that any teacher is ever going to have to worry about.

Even the best teachers fail. Talk to these teachers, and no matter how well the lesson went, they always can think of things that didn't go as well as they would have liked, things that they will do differently next time. But things get much, much worse when we collect the students' notebooks and look at what they thought we said. That's why Doug Lemov (2010) says that, for teachers, no amount of success is enough. The only teachers who think they are successful are those who have low expectations of their students. They are the sort of teachers who say, "What can you expect from these kids?" The answer is, of course, a lot more than the students are achieving with those teachers. The best teachers fail all the time because they have such high aspirations for what their students can achieve (generally much higher than the students themselves have).

I am often contacted by people who ask me whether I have any research instruments for evaluating the quality of teaching. I don't, because working out which teachers are good and which teachers are not so good is of far less interest to me than helping teachers improve. No teacher is so good—or so bad—that he or she cannot improve. That is why we need professional development.

Although there is widespread agreement that professional development is valuable, there is much less agreement about what form it should take, and there is little research about what should be the focus of teacher professional development. However, there is consensus that the "one-shot deals"—sessions ranging from one to five days held during the summer—are of limited effectiveness, even though they are the most common model. The following sections highlight some of the more popular areas of focus for professional development.

Learning Styles

Many teachers have been attracted to developments such as theories pertaining to learning styles. The idea that each learner has a particular preferred style of learning is attractive—intuitive even. It marries up with every teacher's experience that students really are different; it just feels right. However, there is little agreement among psychologists about what learning styles are, let alone how they should be defined. Indeed, it is difficult not to get the impression that the proposers of new classifications of learning styles have followed Annette Karmiloff-Smith's advice: "If you want to get ahead, get a theory" (Karmiloff-Smith & Inhelder, 1974/1975). Some of the definitions, and the questionnaires used to measure them, are so flaky that the same individual will be classified as having one learning style one day and a different one the next (Boyle, 1995). Others do seem to tap into deep and stable differences between individuals in how they think and learn, but there does not appear to be any way to use this in teaching.

Although a number of studies have tried to show that taking students' individual learning styles into account improves learning, evidence remains elusive. There are studies that have shown that being forced to learn in a style different from one's preferred learning style can lead to deeper and more lasting learning. Folding your arms in your preferred way feels effortless and natural, and folding your arms the opposite way feels awkward and unnatural. And yet, for many people, not until they are asked to fold their arms the opposite way do they realise what is involved in folding their arms.

A review of the literature on learning styles and learning strategies (Adey, Fairbrother, Wiliam, Johnson & Jones, 1999) concluded that:

> The only feasible "solution" is that teachers should NOT try to fit their teaching to each child's style, but rather that they should become aware of different styles (and help students also to become aware of different styles) and then encourage all students to use as wide a variety of styles as possible. Students need to learn both how to make the best of their own learning style and also how to use a variety of styles, and to understand the dangers of taking a limited view of their own capabilities. (p. 36)

Educational Neuroscience

Another potential area for teacher professional development—one that has received a lot of publicity in recent years—is concerned with applying what we are learning about the brain to the design of effective teaching. Cognitive psychologists work to understand what the brain does and how the brain does what it does, while neuroscientists try to connect what the brain does to its physiology.

Some of the earliest attempts to relate brain physiology to educational matters were related to the respective roles of the left and right sides of the brain in various kinds of tasks in education and training despite clear evidence that the conclusions being drawn were unwarranted (see, for example, Hines, 1987). More recently, schools have been inundated with suggestions for how they can use the latest findings from cognitive neuroscience to develop "brain-based education", and despite the wealth of evidence that these claims are at best premature and at worst simply disingenuous (for example, Bruer, 1997, 1999; Goswami, 2006; Howard-Jones, 2009), many "neuromyths" still abound.

Content Area Knowledge

If training teachers in cognitive neuroscience isn't going to help, what about increasing teachers' knowledge of their subjects? After all, surely the more teachers know about their subjects, the more their students will learn.

There is evidence that teachers in countries that are more successful in international comparisons than the United States appear to have stronger knowledge of the subjects they are teaching (Ma, 1999; Babcock et al., 2010), and this, at least in part, appears to be responsible for a widespread belief that teacher professional development needs to be focused on teachers' knowledge of the subject matter they are teaching.

Summer professional development workshops do increase teachers' knowledge of their subjects (Hill & Ball, 2004), and as we saw in chapter 1, students do learn more with more knowledgeable teachers (Hill, Rowan & Ball, 2005), although the effects are small. The difficulty with such research findings is that we don't know whether the effects are causal or not. Perhaps the teachers with greater subject knowledge are just smarter, and that's what makes the difference, rather than the subject knowledge. What we do know is that attempts to increase student achievement by increasing teachers' subject knowledge have shown very disappointing results.

An evaluation of professional development designed to improve year-two teachers' reading instruction found that an eight-day content-focused workshop did increase teachers' knowledge of scientifically based reading instruction and also improved the teachers' classroom practices on one out of three instructional practices that had been emphasised in the professional development (Garet et al., 2008). However, at the end of the following school year, there was no impact on the students' reading test scores. More surprisingly, even when the workshop was supplemented with in-school coaching, the effects were the same.

A similar story emerges from an evaluation of professional development for middle years maths teachers in seventy-seven schools in twelve regions (Garet et al., 2010). The program was implemented as intended and resulted in an average of fifty-five hours of additional professional development for participants (who had been selected by lottery). Although the professional development had been specifically designed to be relevant to the curricula that the teachers were using in their classrooms and did have some impact on teachers' classroom practice (specifically the extent to which they engaged in activities that elicited student thinking), there was no impact on student achievement, even in the specific areas on which the intervention focused (ratio, proportion, fractions, percentages and decimals).

These findings are clearly counterintuitive. It seems obvious that teachers need to know about the subjects they are teaching, and yet, the relationship between teachers' knowledge of the subjects and their students' progress is weak, and attempts to improve student outcomes by increasing teachers' subject knowledge appear to be almost entirely failures.

Of course, these failures could be due to our inability to capture the kinds of subject knowledge that are necessary for good teaching, but they suggest that there is much more to good teaching than knowing the subject. We know that teachers make a difference, but we know much less about what makes the difference in teachers. However, there is a body of literature that shows a large impact on student achievement across different subjects, across different age groups and across different countries, and that is the research on formative assessment.

The Origins of Formative Assessment

The term *formative evaluation* was first used in 1967 by Michael Scriven to describe the role that evaluation could play "in the on-going improvement of the curriculum" (Scriven, 1967, p. 41). He contrasted this with summative evaluation, which was designed "to enable administrators to decide whether the entire finished curriculum, refined by use of the evaluation process in its first role, represents a sufficiently significant advance on the available alternatives to justify the expense of adoption by a school system" (pp. 41–42).

Two years later, Benjamin Bloom (1969) applied the same distinction to classroom tests:

> Quite in contrast is the use of "formative evaluation" to provide feedback and correctives at each stage in the teaching-learning process. By formative evaluation we mean evaluation by brief tests used by teachers and students as aids in the learning process. While such tests may be graded and used as part of the judging and classificatory function of evaluation, we see much more effective use of formative evaluation if it is separated from the grading process and used primarily as an aid to teaching. (p. 48)

He went on to say, "Evaluation which is directly related to the teaching-learning process as it unfolds can have highly beneficial effects on the learning of students, the instructional process of teachers, and the use of instructional materials by teachers and learners" (Bloom, 1969, p. 50).

Although the term *formative* was little used over the following twenty years, a number of studies investigated ways of integrating assessment with instruction, the best known of which is probably cognitively guided instruction (CGI).

In the original CGI project, a group of twenty-one primary school teachers participated, over a period of four years, in a series of workshops in which the teachers were shown extracts of videotapes selected to illustrate critical aspects of children's thinking. The teachers were then prompted to reflect on what they had seen, by, for example, being challenged to relate the way a child had solved one problem to how she had solved or might solve other problems (Fennema et al., 1996). Throughout the project, the teachers were encouraged to make use of the evidence they had collected about the achievement of their students to adjust their instruction to better meet their students' learning needs. Students taught by CGI teachers did better in number fact knowledge, understanding, problem solving and confidence (Carpenter, Fennema, Peterson, Chiang & Loef, 1989), and four years after the end of the program, the participating teachers were still implementing the principles of the program (Franke, Carpenter, Levi & Fennema, 2001).

The power of using assessment to adapt instruction is vividly illustrated in a study of the implementation of the measurement and planning system (MAPS), in which twenty-nine teachers, each with an aide and a site manager, assessed the readiness for learning of 428 kindergarten students. The students were tested in maths and reading in autumn and again in spring. Their teachers were trained to interpret the test results and provided with the *Classroom Activity Library*—a series of activities typical of early years instruction but tied specifically to empirically validated developmental progressions—that they could use to individualise instruction. The performances of these students were then compared with the performances of 410 other students taught by twenty-seven other teachers. At the end of the year, 27 per cent of the students in the control group were referred for placement and 20 per cent were actually placed into special education programs for the following year. In the MAPS group, only 6 per cent were referred, and less than 2 per cent were placed in special education programs.

In addition to these specific studies, a number of research reviews were beginning to highlight the importance of using assessment to inform instruction. A review by Lynn Fuchs and Douglas Fuchs (1986) synthesised findings from twenty-one different research studies on the use of assessment to inform the instruction of students with special needs. They found that regular assessment (two to five times per week) with follow-up action produced a substantial increase in student learning. When teachers set rules about how they would review the data and the actions that were to follow before they assessed their students, the gains in achievement were twice as great as those cases in which the follow-up action was left to the judgment of the individual's teacher once the data had been collected. Interestingly, when teachers produced graphs of the progress of individual students as a guide and stimulus to action, the effect was almost three times as great as when this was not done.

Over the next two years, two further research reviews, one by Gary Natriello (1987) and the other by Terence Crooks (1988), provided clear evidence that classroom assessment had a substantial—and usually negative—impact on student learning. Natriello's major finding was that much of the research he reviewed was difficult to interpret because of a failure to make key distinctions (for example, between the quality and quantity of feedback) in the design of the research, so although it was clear that assessment could be harmful, it was not clear why. Crooks' paper focused specifically on the impact of assessment practices on students and concluded that although classroom assessments did have the power to influence learning, too often the use of assessments for summative purposes got in the way.

In 1998, Paul Black and I sought to update the reviews of Natriello and Crooks. One of the immediate difficulties that we encountered was how to define the field of study. The reviews by Natriello and Crooks had cited 91 and 241 references, respectively, and yet only 9 references were common to both papers, and neither had cited the review by Fuchs and Fuchs. Rather than rely on electronic search methods, we resorted to a manual search of each issue between 1987 and 1997 of seventy-six journals we thought would be most likely to contain relevant research. In the end, we identified a total of just over 600 potentially relevant studies, of which around 250 were directly relevant.

Because the range of studies was so broad, we did not attempt a meta-analysis. Instead, we tried to make sense of the research we had found. We concluded that the research suggested that attention to the use of assessment to inform instruction, particularly at the classroom level, in many cases effectively doubled the speed of student learning. We realised that because of the diversity of the studies, there was no simple recipe that could be easily applied in every classroom, but we were confident we had identified some fruitful avenues for further exploration:

> Despite the existence of some marginal and even negative results, the range of conditions and contexts under which studies have shown that gains can be achieved must indicate that the principles that underlie achievement of substantial improvements in learning are robust. Significant gains can be achieved by many different routes, and initiatives here are not likely to fail through neglect of delicate and subtle features. (Black & Wiliam, 1998a, pp. 61–62)

In order to explore how these research findings could be implemented in typical classrooms, we worked with a group of twenty-four (later expanded to thirty-six) secondary school mathematics and science teachers in six schools in two districts in England (Black, Harrison, Lee, Marshall & Wiliam, 2003).

The work with teachers had two main components. The first was a series of eight workshops over an eighteen-month period in which teachers were introduced to the research base underlying how assessment can support learning, had the opportunity to develop their own plans for implementing formative assessment practices, and, at later meetings, could discuss with colleagues the changes they had attempted to make in their practice. Most of the teachers' plans contained reference to two or three important areas in their teaching in which they were seeking to increase their use of formative assessment, generally followed by details of techniques that would be used to make this happen.

The second component was a series of visits by researchers to the teachers' classrooms, so that the teachers could be observed implementing some of the ideas they had discussed in the workshops and could discuss how their ideas could be put into practice more effectively.

Because each teacher had made his own decisions about what aspect of formative assessment to emphasise and which classes to try it with, it was impossible to use a traditional experimental design to evaluate the effects of our intervention. Therefore, we designed a "poly-experiment". For each class with which a teacher was trying out formative assessment techniques, we looked for the most similar comparison class and set up a mini-experiment in which the test scores of the class that was using formative assessment were compared with the test scores of the comparison class. This experimental design is not as good as a random-allocation trial, because the teachers participating in the experiment might have been better teachers to begin with, and so the results need to be interpreted with some caution. Nevertheless, in this study, using scores on externally scored standardised tests, the students with which the teachers used formative assessment techniques made almost twice as much progress over the year (Wiliam, Lee, Harrison & Black, 2004).

What, Exactly, Is Formative Assessment?

As the evidence that formative assessment can have a significant impact on student learning has accumulated, a variety of definitions of *formative assessment* has been proposed. In our original review, Paul Black and I defined *formative assessment* "as encompassing all those activities undertaken by teachers, and/or by their students, which provide information to be used as feedback to modify the teaching and learning activities in which they are engaged" (Black & Wiliam, 1998a, p. 7). Writing around the same time, Bronwen Cowie and Beverley Bell qualified this slightly by requiring that the information from the assessment be acted upon while learning was taking place. They defined *formative assessment* as "the process used by teachers and students to recognise and respond to student learning in order to enhance that learning, *during the learning*" (Cowie & Bell, 1999, p. 32, emphasis added). Others have also emphasised the need for action during instruction and defined *formative assessment* as "assessment carried out during the instructional process for the purpose of improving teaching or learning" (Shepard et al., 2005, p. 275). A review of practice by the OECD across eight countries defined *formative assessment* as "frequent, interactive assessments of students' progress and understanding to identify learning needs and adjust teaching appropriately" (Looney, 2005, p. 21).

What is notable about these definitions is that, however implicitly, formative assessment is regarded as a process. Others have tended to regard formative assessment as a tool. For example, Stuart Kahl (2005) defined formative assessment as "a tool that teachers use to measure student grasp of specific topics and skills they are teaching. It's a 'midstream' tool to identify specific student misconceptions and mistakes while the material is being taught" (p. 11). Indeed, it appears that the term *formative assessment* is now more often used to refer to a particular kind of assessment instrument than a process by which instruction might be improved.

The difficulty with trying to make the term *formative assessment* apply to a thing (the assessment itself) is that it just does not work. Consider an AP calculus teacher who is getting her students ready to take their examination. Like many teachers, she has her students take a practice examination under formal test conditions. Most teachers would then collect the papers, score them, write comments for the students, and return the papers to the students so that they could see where they went wrong. However, this calculus teacher does something slightly different. She collects the papers at the end of the examination, but she does not score them. Instead, during her next period with the class, each group of four students receives their unscored papers and one blank examination paper, and has to compile the best composite examination paper response that they can. Within each group, the students review their responses, comparing their answers to each question and discussing what the best answer would be. Toward the end of the period, the teacher reviews the activity with the whole class, asking each group to share with the rest of the class their agreed answers.

The assessment that the teacher used—an AP calculus examination—was designed entirely for summative purposes. AP exams are designed by the College Board to confer college-level credit so that students passing the exam at a suitable level are exempt from introductory courses in university. However, this teacher used the assessment instrument formatively—what Black and I have called "formative use of summative tests". Describing an assessment as formative is, in fact, what Gilbert Ryle (1949) called a "category error": the error of ascribing to something a property that it cannot have, like describing a rock as happy. Because the same assessment can be used both formatively and summatively, the terms *formative* and *summative* make much more sense as descriptions of the function that assessment data serve, rather than of the assessments themselves (Wiliam & Black, 1996).

Some people (for example, Popham, 2006; Shepard, 2008) have called for the term *formative assessment* not to be used at all, unless instruction is improved. In the United Kingdom, the Assessment Reform Group argued that using assessment to improve learning required five elements to be in place:

1. The provision of effective feedback to students

2. The active involvement of students in their own learning

3. The adjustment of teaching to take into account the results of assessment

4. The recognition of the profound influence assessment has on the motivation and self-esteem of students, both of which are crucial influences on learning

5. The need for students to be able to assess themselves and understand how to improve

They suggested that *formative assessment*—at least in the way many people used it—was not a helpful term for describing such uses of assessment because "the term 'formative' itself is open to a variety of interpretations and often means no more than that assessment is carried out frequently and is planned at the same time as teaching" (Broadfoot, et al., 1999, p. 7). Instead, they suggested that it would be better to use the phrase *assessment for learning,* which had first been used by Harry Black (1986) and was brought to a wider audience by Mary James at the 1992 annual meeting of the ASCD in New Orleans.

Rick Stiggins (2005) has since popularised the use of the term *assessment* for *learning* in North America and has argued that it is very different from what has historically been regarded as "formative assessment":

> If formative assessment is about more frequent, assessment
> FOR learning is about continuous. If formative assessment is
> about providing teachers with evidence, assessment FOR
> learning is about informing the students themselves. If formative

assessment tells users who is and who is not meeting state standards, assessment FOR learning tells them what progress each student is making toward meeting each standard while the learning is happening—when there's still time to be helpful. (pp. 1–2)

However, just replacing the term *formative assessment* with the term *assessment for learning* merely clouds the definitional issue (Bennett, 2009). What really matters is what kind of processes we value, not what we call them. The problem, as Randy Bennett (2009) points out, is that it is an oversimplification to say that formative assessment is *only* a matter of process or *only* a matter of instrumentation. Good processes require good instruments, and instruments are useless unless they are used intelligently.

The original, literal meaning of the word *formative* suggests that formative assessments should shape instruction—our formative experiences are those that have shaped our current selves—and so we need a definition that can accommodate all the ways in which assessment can shape instruction. And there are many. Consider the following scenarios:

1. In spring 2009, a mathematics curriculum supervisor needs to plan the 2010 summer workshops that will be offered to middle years maths teachers in the region. She analyses the scores obtained by the regions' middle years students in the 2009 national tests and notes that while the maths scores are generally comparable to those of the rest of the state, the students in her region appear to be scoring rather poorly on items involving ratio and proportion. She decides to make ratio and proportion the focus of the professional development activities offered in summer 2010, which are well attended by the region's middle years maths teachers. Teachers return to school in summer 2010 and use the revised instructional methods they have developed. As a result, when the students take the national test in 2011, the achievement of middle years students in the region on items involving ratio and proportion increases, and so the region's performance on the national tests, improves.

2. Each year, a group of secondary school teachers of Algebra I review students' performance on a statewide Algebra I test and, in particular, look at the facility (proportion correct) for each

item on the test. When item facilities are lower than expected, they look at how instruction on that aspect of the curriculum was planned and delivered, and they look at ways in which the instruction can be strengthened in the following year.

3. A school region uses a series of interim tests that are tied to the curriculum and administered at intervals of six to ten weeks to check on student progress. Students whose scores are below the threshold determined from past experience to be necessary to have an 80 per cent chance of passing the national test are required to attend additional instruction on Saturday mornings.

4. A middle years science teacher is designing a unit on pulleys and levers. Fourteen periods are allocated to the unit, but all the content is covered in the first eleven periods. Building on ideas common in Japan (Lewis, 2002), in period 12, the teacher gives the students a quiz and collects the papers. Instead of marking the papers, she reads through them carefully, and on the basis of what she discovers about what the class has and has not learned, she plans appropriate remedial activity for periods 13 and 14.

5. A history teacher has been teaching about the issue of bias in historical sources. Three minutes before the end of the lesson, students pack away their books and are given an index card on which they are asked to respond to the question "Why are historians concerned about bias in historical sources?" The students hand in these exit passes as they leave the class at the end of the period. After all the students have left, the teacher reads through the cards and then discards them, having concluded that the students' answers indicate a good enough understanding for the teacher to move on to a new chapter.

6. An English teacher has been teaching her students about different kinds of figurative language. Before moving on, she wants to check her students' understanding of the terms she has been teaching, so she uses a real-time test. She gives each student a set of six cards bearing the letters A, B, C, D, E and F, and on the board, she displays the following:

A. Alliteration

B. Onomatopoeia

C. Hyperbole

D. Personification

E. Simile

F. Metaphor

She then reads a series of statements:

- This backpack weighs a tonne.

- He was as tall as a house.

- The sweetly smiling sunshine melted all the snow.

- He honked his horn at the cyclist.

- He was a bull in a china shop.

After the teacher reads each statement, she asks the class to hold up a letter card (or cards) to indicate which kind(s) of figurative language features in the statement. All students respond correctly to the first question, but in responding to the second, each student holds up a single card (some hold up E, and some hold up C). The teacher reminds the class that some of the statements might be more than a single type of figurative language. Once they realise that there can be more than one answer, the class responds correctly to statements 2, 3 and 4. About half the students, however, indicate that they think statement 5 is a simile. The teacher then leads a whole-class discussion during which students give their reasons for why they think statement 5 is a simile or a metaphor, and after a few minutes, all the students agree that it is a metaphor, because it does not include *like* or *as*.

7. An maths teacher has been teaching students about graph sketching and wants to check quickly that the students have grasped the main principles. She asks the students, "Please sketch the graph of y equals one over one plus x squared." Each

student sketches the graph on a whiteboard and holds it up for the teacher to see. The teacher sees that the class has understood and moves on.

In each of these seven examples, evidence of student achievement was elicited, interpreted and used to make a decision about what to do next. In most, the decision was made to adjust the instruction to better meet the learning needs of the class, and the assessment allowed the teacher or teachers to make smarter decisions than would have been possible had they not collected the evidence. In examples 5 and 7, however, the teacher discovered that the students had understood what she wanted them to learn well enough for them to move on; the decision was that no adjustment was necessary.

Each can be considered an example of formative assessment. In the first example, the length of the cycle is over two years; in the second, it's a year; in the third, it's a few weeks; and in the fourth and fifth, it's a matter of one or two days. The last two are even shorter, taking place in real time within a single period. A good definition of *formative assessment* will have to admit all of these as examples of formative assessment, and it is unlikely that any definition will command universal agreement. Nevertheless, having spent a lot of time pondering this, I think the following definition works pretty well:

> An assessment functions formatively to the extent that evidence about student achievement is elicited, interpreted and used by teachers, learners or their peers to make decisions about the next steps in instruction that are likely to be better, or better founded, than the decisions they would have made in the absence of that evidence.

The first point to make about this definition is that the term *formative* is used to describe the function that evidence from the assessment actually serves, rather than the assessment itself.

The second point concerns who is actually doing the assessment. While in many cases, the decisions will be made by the teacher, the definition also includes individual learners or their peers as agents in making such decisions.

The third point is that the focus is on decisions instead of on the intentions of those involved, as is the case with some definitions of *assessment for learning.* Evidence that is collected with the intent of being used but never actually used is unhelpful.

The fourth point continues the third. As an alternative to focusing the definition on the intent, we could focus on the resulting *action*. In other words, we could require that the evidence be used to make adjustments that actually improve learning beyond what would have happened without those adjustments. This, however, would be too stringent. Learning is just too unpredictable for us ever to guarantee that learning will take place on a particular occasion. Moreover, if we required the assessment to result in better learning than would have occurred in the absence of the assessment, it would be impossible to establish that any assessment was ever formative, since we would need to establish a counterclaim: that what actually happened was different (and better than) what would otherwise have happened (but did not). The probabilistic formulation (that the decisions are *likely* to be better) reflects the fact that even the best-designed interventions will not *always* result in better learning for *all* students.

The fifth point is that the focus is on decisions about the next steps in *instruction*. In much of the English-speaking world, the word *instruction* has a connotation of training or of "transmission" approaches to teaching. Here, the term *instruction* refers to the combination of teaching and learning, to any activity that is intended to create learning (defined as an increase, brought about by experience, in the capacities of an individual to act in valued ways).

The sixth point is that decisions are *either* better *or* better founded than decisions that would have been made without the evidence elicited as part of the assessment process. The second possibility is included because the formative assessment might, as we saw in the fifth and seventh examples, indicate to the teacher that the best course of action is what the teacher had intended to do all along. The formative assessment might not change the course of action but instead simply show that the proposed course of action was right.

The emphasis on decisions as being at the heart of formative assessment also assists with the design of the assessment process. With many so-called formative assessments, assessment data are generated and then communicated to teachers with the expectation that teachers will be able to use the information in some way.

However, if the formative assessments are designed without any clear decision in mind, then there is a good chance that the information from the assessment will be useless. For example, many vendors now offer schools regular student testing (typically every four to ten weeks), and the results are fed back to the teachers. Sometimes these results are reported simply in terms of which students are on target to reach proficiency on national tests, but even when the results are more detailed, they are often of little use to the teachers for two reasons. First, the results are usually at the level of national standards, which are generally too coarse to guide teachers' instructional decision making. Second, the results usually arrive weeks after the teacher has moved on. Caroline Wylie and I describe this kind of formative assessment as "data-push" (Wylie & Wiliam, 2006). Data are pushed at teachers, and although those designing the assessments aren't really clear about what the teacher should do with the information, the teacher is expected to be able to make some use of the data.

The alternative is to design the assessments backward from the decisions. When the focus is on the decision that needs to be made, the teacher can then look at relevant sources of evidence that would contribute to making that decision in a smarter way. With such a "decision-pull" approach, the teacher always knows what to do with the data once they are collected because that has been thought through *before* the data were collected.

Strategies of Formative Assessment

The discussion thus far has established that any assessment can be formative and that assessment functions formatively when it improves the instructional decisions that are made by teachers, learners or their peers. These decisions can be immediate, on-the-fly decisions or longer term. However, if we want to really see what formative assessment looks like on the ground, we have to dig a little deeper.

All teaching really boils down to three key processes and three kinds of individuals involved. The processes are: finding out where learners are in their learning, finding out where they are going and finding out how to get there. The roles are: teacher, learner and peer. Crossing the roles with the processes gives us a three-by-three grid of nine cells, which can be grouped into five "key strategies" of formative assessment with one big idea (Leahy, Lyon, Thompson & Wiliam, 2005), as shown in figure

2.2. The five key strategies are:

1. Clarifying, sharing and understanding learning intentions and criteria for success

2. Engineering effective classroom discussions, activities and learning tasks that elicit evidence of learning

3. Providing feedback that moves learning forward

4. Activating learners as instructional resources for one another

5. Activating learners as the owners of their own learning

The big idea is that evidence about learning is used to adjust instruction to better meet student needs—in other words, teaching is *adaptive* to the learner's needs. Over the next five chapters, each of these strategies is discussed in greater detail. Before moving on, however, it is worth considering why assessment should occupy such a central position in teaching.

	Where the learner is going	Where the learner is right now	How to get there
Teacher	Clarifying and sharing learning intentions and criteria for success	Engineering effective classroom discussions, activities and tasks that elicit evidence of learning	Providing feedback that moves learning forward
Peer	Understanding and sharing learning intentions and criteria for success	Activating learners as instructional resources for one another	
Learner	Understanding learning intentions and criteria for success	Activating learners as the owners of their own learning	

Figure 2.2: The five key strategies of formative assessment. Adapted from Leahy, Lyon, Thompson, & Wiliam, 2005.

Assessment: The Bridge Between Teaching and Learning

Assessment occupies such a central position in good teaching because we cannot predict what students will learn, no matter how we design our teaching. In a very carefully designed experiment, Brenda Denvir developed a detailed taxonomy of children's early number skills and showed that some were prerequisites for others (Denvir & Brown, 1986a). For example, she found that before students could subtract one single-digit number from another, they needed to be able to count backward by one (in other words, be able to name the number immediately preceding a given number).

One student—called Jy in the study—had specific knowledge "gaps" in the following areas:

- Knows the numbers backward from twenty
- Knows number bonds (not just the "doubles")
- Knows the answer when adding units to a decade number
- Knows the answer when adding ten to a two-digit number
- Knows the answer when taking ten away from a two-digit number

Over two months, Jy's teacher planned and delivered specific instruction to address these gaps, and at the end of the process, Jy was assessed again.

Surprisingly, on the post-test, Jy could not demonstrate mastery of any of the skills that she had been specifically taught, although on a delayed post-test (five months later), she did show mastery of one of the taught skills ("Knows the answer when adding units to a decade number"). However, in the post-test, she did show mastery of a number of other skills that she had not demonstrated on the pre-test:

- Uses counting up/back/down strategy for "take-away"
- Models two-digit addition without regrouping using base-ten apparatus
- Models two-digit subtraction without regrouping using base-ten apparatus
- Models two-digit addition with regrouping using base-ten apparatus
- Bundles objects to make new groups of ten in order to facilitate enumeration of a collection that is partly grouped in tens and ones

The skills that Jy acquired were consistent with the hierarchies that Denvir had identified—they just weren't the skills her teacher had taught, and the same was found to be true for other students in the study (Brown & Denvir, 1986b).

This is why assessment is *the* central process in instruction. Students do not learn what we teach. If they did, we would not need to keep mark-books. We could, instead, simply record what we have taught. But anyone who has spent any time in a classroom knows that what students learn as a result of our instruction is unpredictable. We teach what we think are good lessons, but then, after we collect our students' notebooks, we wonder how they could have misinterpreted what we said so completely.

The truth is that we often mix up teaching and learning, as the following old joke shows:

> Amy: I taught my dog to whistle.
> Betty: Let's hear it then.
> Amy: He can't whistle.
> Betty: I thought you said you taught him to whistle.
> Amy: I did. He just didn't learn it.

At one time, school inspectors in England claimed to be able to distinguish between the quality of teaching and the quality of learning in a classroom, although it is hard to work out what the basis of such a distinction might be. After all, what sense does it make to talk about a lesson for which the quality of teaching was high but the quality of learning was low? It's rather like a surgeon claiming that an operation was a complete success, but unfortunately, the patient died.

In some languages, the distinction between teaching and learning is impossible to make—in Welsh and Māori, for example, the same word is used for both (*dysgu* and *ako*, respectively). In languages where it is possible to distinguish teaching from learning, however, the phrase *teaching and learning* is in many cases being replaced by the phrase *learning and teaching* (although the former still gets three times as many Google hits as the latter).

This is often touted as a "good move", as if putting the word *learning* before the word *teaching* makes a difference, but it is largely a cosmetic change, and one that could actually be harmful, because it draws attention to rather trivial differences, leaving much more important issues obscured. To say that learning is more important than teaching is a bit like saying that travelling is more important than driving. Travelling is the goal, and driving is a way to achieve that goal. In the same way, student learning is the goal, and teaching is a way to achieve that goal. And in the same way that drivers achieve their goal (travelling) by driving, teachers achieve their goal (student learning) by teaching.

Every action that a teacher takes, provided it is intended to result in student learning, is teaching, but the teacher cannot do the learning for the learner; teaching is all the teacher can do. The trap is thinking that this is the end point rather than a means to an end. As one teacher put it:

> Actually thinking about teaching has meant that I have been able to come up with ideas and strategies to cope with whatever has arisen and has contributed greatly to my professional development. I now think more about the content of the lesson. The influence has shifted from "what am I going to teach and what are the pupils going to do?" towards "how am I going to teach this and what are the pupils going to learn?" (Black, Harrison, Lee, Marshall & Wiliam, 2004, p. 19)

This is, in practice, a very difficult course to steer. At one extreme, there are teachers who try to do the learning for the learners, epitomised by the old joke that schools are places where children go to watch teachers work. I visit a lot of classrooms, and in most of them, the teacher is working really hard, but the students? Not so much. That is why I often say to teachers, "If your students are going home at the end of the day less tired than you are, the division of labour in your classroom requires some attention."

At the other extreme are the teachers who use the F-word—facilitate. "I don't teach," they say. "I just facilitate learning." I am never quite sure what this means. Presumably, the teachers are just hanging around, hoping that some learning will occur.

Teaching is difficult because neither of these extremes is acceptable. When the pressure is on, most of us behave as if lecturing works, but deep down, we know it's ineffective. But leaving the students to discover everything for themselves is equally inappropriate. For this reason, I describe teaching as the engineering of effective learning environments. And sometimes, a teacher does her best teaching before the students arrive in the classroom.

Many teachers have had the experience of creating an effective group discussion task in which the students engage completely in a really tricky challenge that they must resolve. The only problem is there is nothing for the teacher to do. He feels a little bored and a tad guilty that he is not doing anything, so he disrupts a group's work. This is one version of what I call the teaching-learning trap: I'm not doing anything; therefore, the students can't be learning anything. The other version of the trap was discussed earlier: I am working hard, so the students must be learning something.

The teacher's job is not to transmit knowledge, nor to facilitate learning. It is to engineer effective learning environments for the students. The key features of effective learning environments are that they create student engagement and allow teachers, learners and their peers to ensure that the learning is proceeding in the intended direction. The only way we can do this is through assessment. That is why assessment is, indeed, the bridge between teaching and learning.

Conclusion

In this chapter, we learned that the regular use of minute-by-minute and day-by-day classroom formative assessment can substantially improve student achievement. Although many different definitions of formative assessment have been proposed, the essential idea is simple. Teaching is a *contingent* activity. We cannot predict what students will learn as a result of any particular sequence of instruction. Formative assessment involves getting the best possible evidence about what students have learned and then using this information to decide what to do next.

There are five key strategies of formative assessment. The next five chapters probe each of these five strategies in more depth, offering details of research studies that provide evidence of their importance and a number of practical techniques that can be used to implement the strategies in classrooms.

CHAPTER 3

Clarifying, Sharing and Understanding Learning Intentions and Success Criteria

It seems obvious that students might find it helpful to know what they are going to be learning, and yet, consistently sharing learning intentions with students is a relatively recent phenomenon in most classrooms. This chapter reviews some of the research evidence on the effects of ensuring learners understand what they are meant to be doing and explains why it is helpful to distinguish between learning intentions, the context of the learning and success criteria. The chapter also provides a number of techniques that teachers can use to share learning intentions and success criteria with their students.

Why Learning Intentions Are Important

Back in 1971, Mary Alice White tried to imagine "the view from the student's desk":

> The analogy that might make the student's view more comprehensible to adults is to imagine oneself on a ship sailing across an unknown sea, to an unknown destination. An adult would be

> desperate to know where he is going. But a child only knows he is going to school . . . The chart is neither available nor understandable to him . . . Very quickly, the daily life on board ship becomes all important . . . The daily chores, the demands, the inspections, become the reality, not the voyage, nor the destination. (p. 340)

Not all students have the same idea as their teachers about what they are meant to be doing in the classroom. For a simple example, we might ask students which is the odd one out in the following list of objects: knife, fork, hammer, bottle of ketchup. Some students will say that the bottle of ketchup is the odd one out, because the others are all metal tools. Other students will say that the hammer is the odd one out because the other objects can be found on their kitchen table at mealtime. Of course, in an absolute sense, neither of these two answers is better than the other, but as Nell Keddie (1971) pointed out years ago, schools place a greater value on the first way of thinking about the world than the second. Sometimes this is made explicit—most students probably realise that being able to name all the Prime Ministers of Australia is valued more in school than being able to name the team roster for the Carlton football team, even though both of these tasks are comparable in length. But often, what is wanted is not made clear, and this puts some students at a considerable advantage *because they already know*.

If I show a piece of writing to a group of year three students and ask them why I think it's a good piece of writing, some will respond with contributions like, "It's got lots of descriptive adjectives," "It's got strong verbs," or "It uses lots of different transition words." Others will suggest that I think the work is good "because it's neat and long," reminiscent of the teacher Paul Pennyfeather in Evelyn Waugh's *Decline and Fall* who instructs his class, "Meanwhile, you will write an essay on 'self-indulgence.' There will be a prize for the longest essay, irrespective of any possible merit" (Waugh, 2001, p. 38).

A number of research studies have highlighted the importance of students understanding what they are meant to be doing. Eddie Gray and David Tall (1994) looked at the mathematical reasoning skills of seventy-two students between the ages of seven and thirteen. They found that higher-achieving students were able to work with unresolved ambiguities about what they were doing, while those students seen as lower achieving were struggling because they were trying to do something much more difficult.

To illustrate this, I often ask teachers to write $4x$ and $4\frac{1}{2}$. I then ask them what the mathematical operation is between the 4 and the x, which most realise is multiplication. I then ask what the operation is between the 4 and the $\frac{1}{2}$, which is, of course, addition. I then ask whether any of them had previously noticed this inconsistency in mathematical notation—that when numbers are next to each other, sometimes it means multiply, sometimes it means add, and sometimes it means something completely different, as when we write a two-digit number like 43. Most teachers have never noticed this inconsistency, which presumably is how they were able to be successful at school. The student who worries about this and asks the teacher why mathematical notation is inconsistent in this regard may be told not to ask stupid questions, even though this is a rather intelligent question and displays exactly the kind of curiosity that might be useful for a mathematician—but he has to get through school first!

A vivid illustration of the power of understanding what you are meant to be doing was provided by a study of twelve science classrooms in two urban middle years schools in the United States (White & Frederiksen, 1998). Seven of the classrooms were year seven; three were year eight; and two were year nine. Each class (average size of thirty students) had one forty-five-minute science period each school day.

All twelve classes followed the ThinkerTools curriculum—designed to promote thinking in the science classroom—for approximately eleven weeks, during which time they covered seven modules:

Module 1. One-dimensional motion

Module 2. Friction

Module 3. Mass project (the Common Inquiry Project)

Module 4. Two-dimensional motion

Module 5. Gravity

Module 6. Trajectories

Module 7. Final project (the Chosen Inquiry Project)

Each module incorporated a series of evaluation activities. In six of the classes (selected at random to act as a control group), these evaluation episodes took the form of a discussion, once each week, about what the students liked and disliked about the topic. In the other six classes, once a week, students engaged in a process of reflective assessment. Through a series of small-group and individual activities, the students were introduced to the nine assessment criteria (each of which was assessed on a five-point scale) that the teacher would use to evaluate their work. At the end of each episode within a module, the students were asked to assess their performance against two of the criteria. At the end of the module, students had to assess their performance against all nine. For each assessment, they had to write a brief statement showing which aspects of their work formed the basis for their rating. Students presented their work to the class, and their peers used the criteria to give them feedback.

All the students in the study also took the Comprehensive Tests of Basic Skills (CTBS)—a test of basic literacy and numeracy—to check that the treatment groups and the control groups were evenly matched in terms of prior achievement (which they were). At the end of module 3, students completed a project that was scored on a five-point scale. The students' results, classified according to whether the students in each group had scored in the upper or lower half of their class on the CTBS, are shown in table 3.1.

Table 3.1: Mass Project Scores for Students, by Group and CTBS Scores

	Lower half CTBS scores	Upper half CTBS scores
Likes and dislikes (control)	1.9	3.4
Reflective assessment	3.0	3.5

There are two important features of the data in table 3.1. First, the average scores of the students in the reflective assessment classrooms are higher than those in the control group. Although this difference is not significant for those students scoring highly on the CTBS, it shows that high-scoring students were not penalised by being in the reflective assessment group. Second, and more important, in the reflective assessment group, the achievement gap between high scorers and low scorers on the CTBS has been cut by two-thirds, compared with the likes and dislikes classes (average of 0.5 points, compared with 1.5 points).

On the final project, the students were given a score out of 100 for the skills of science inquiry they had demonstrated, which were compared with those they had shown in a pre-test at the beginning of the study. The results are shown in table 3.2.

Table 3.2: Final Inquiry Test Scores for Students, by Group and CTBS Scores

	Pre-test		Post-test	
	Lower	Higher	Lower	Higher
Likes and dislikes (control)	32	59	39	68
Reflective assessment	28	52	53	72

These are rather surprising results, because the difference between the likes and dislikes classes and the reflective assessment classes was not great—just a difference in emphasis in one lesson a week—and yet the changes were radical. In the likes and dislikes group, the high achievers improved by nine points and the low achievers improved by seven points. However, in the reflective assessment group, the high achievers improved by twenty points and the low achievers improved by thirty-five points. Everyone did better in the reflective assessment group, but the magnitude of the benefits was much greater for the lower-achieving students. Some students already know what successful work looks like, and others do not. Ensuring that all students know what quality work looks like has a profound impact on achievement gaps.

Given all this, it is not surprising that Royce Sadler (1989) wrote:

> The indispensable conditions for improvement are that the student comes to hold a concept of quality roughly similar to that held by the teacher, is continuously able to monitor the quality of what is being produced during the act of production itself, and has a repertoire of alternative moves or strategies from which to draw at any given point. (p. 121)

While there could be some discussion about whether, as Sadler claims, any improvement is impossible unless the conditions he specifies are met, there seems to be little doubt that it is a good idea to make sure that students understand the learning intentions behind the activities they undertake in the classroom.

When Are Learning Intentions Useful?

Several regions have mandated that each period of instruction should begin with the teacher posting a learning objective. Indeed, in many regions, teacher evaluation protocols specifically address this by requiring those observing teachers to record whether the lesson objectives have been clearly articulated by the teacher. Too often, the result is a desultory approach to the sharing of learning intentions. The teacher writes the objective on the board; the students copy the objective into their notebooks; and the objective is then ignored for the rest of the period—what has been described as a "wallpaper objective".

This kind of tokenistic approach to the sharing of learning intentions is most definitely not what is intended by the strategy of *clarifying, sharing and understanding learning intentions and success criteria*. As Albert Einstein once said, "Make things as simple as possible, but no simpler." Obviously it's a good idea for students to know where they are going in their learning, but this cannot be done in a formulaic way.

For a start, sometimes it's not even a good idea to tell the students what the lesson is about. Consider the following problem, suitable for a middle years maths class.

Two farmers have inherited adjacent fields with a boundary that has a kink in it:

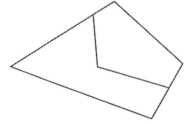

Both farmers find the crooked boundary to be an inconvenience, and so they wonder whether it is possible to divide the two fields with a straight boundary so that each farmer still has the same amount of land.

There are, of course, numerous ways in which such a problem might be solved, but one key insight that simplifies the problem considerably is that triangles with equal bases and the same height must have the same area. So if a straight line is drawn between the points where the boundary meets the edge of the fields, and a parallel line is drawn through the kink in the boundary, any triangles with a base on the line between the boundary points and the third corner on the parallel line will have the same area.

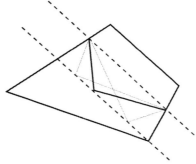

Therefore, either of the two heavy lines on the diagram will do.

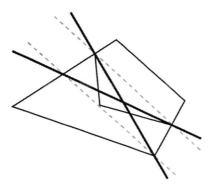

This problem would have been completely pointless if the teacher had told the students at the beginning that they were learning to solve problems involving the area of a triangle. Once one has realised that the area of a triangle is relevant, the problem is relatively simple to solve. Sometimes telling the students where they are going completely spoils the journey! Indeed, in conversations with students, many have said that always being given the objectives at the start of the day turns them off.

At other times, we might be quite comfortable with the idea of giving students clear guidance about what we want, but it turns out to be too difficult. For example, a teacher who is trying to develop her students' ability to engage the attention of the reader might want to spend a period developing the skill of writing an attention-grabbing opening sentence. While this is certainly something that we want students to be able to do, it is questionable whether it is of much help to the students to be told that the day's learning objective is to understand what makes an attention-grabbing opening sentence. The fact that we cannot always put into words what we know is actually a very profound problem, which is too rarely appreciated today, even though it has been recognised for over fifty years.

In his groundbreaking book *Personal Knowledge*, first published in 1958, Michael Polanyi explored the problem of how people come to know things. He pointed out that in many important areas of human affairs, we cannot write down rules for what makes something good, but we can often summarise our perceptions of quality through maxims. However, his key insight was that while maxims are useful to those who already understand what quality means in a specific context, they are useless to those who don't understand what is meant:

> Maxims cannot be understood, still less applied by anyone not already possessing a good practical knowledge of the art. They derive their interest from our appreciation of the art and cannot themselves either replace or establish that appreciation.
> (Polanyi, 1958, p. 50)

More simply, Robert Pirsig, in his sequel to *Zen and the Art of Motorcycle Maintenance*, wrote, "Quality doesn't have to be defined. You understand it without definition. Quality is a direct experience independent of and prior to intellectual abstractions" (Pirsig, 1991, p. 64).

The point that both Polanyi and Pirsig were making is that we sometimes use learning objectives as if they are definitions of quality when in fact they are post-hoc rationalisations of quality, familiar enough to those who know what they are doing but not helpful to those who are not yet there. A friend of mine is a serious golf player, and he told me that for weeks his coach was telling him that he needed to "quieten his lower body". He treated this as guidance about what he needed to work on but found it impossible to make any sense of it. And then, one day, it all clicked. And once it had clicked, the advice made sense. It probably didn't help him achieve the goal, but it did help him know when he had reached it.

In communicating learning intentions to students, therefore, the first thing to decide is whether we are giving, in Polanyi's language, rules or maxims. Sometimes we can be very specific, such as when we require laboratory reports to be structured in a particular way—diagrams are to be drawn in pencil and labelled, and so on. At other times, it may be that the best we can do is help the students develop what Guy Claxton (1995) calls a "nose for quality". Rubrics have a role to play in this process, as they did in the study by Barbara White and Norman Frederiksen.

Rubrics were shared with students, but more important, the students were given time to think through, in discussion with others, what the rubrics might mean in practice, applied to their own work.

It is often valuable to develop the learning intentions jointly with the students—a process that is sometimes called "co-construction". It is important to note that developing learning intentions or success criteria with students is most definitely not a democratic process. The teacher is in a privileged position with respect to the subject being taught and knows more about the subject than the students do, and it would be an abdication of the teacher's responsibilities to let whatever the students feel should be valued be adopted as the learning intentions. The advantage of developing the learning intentions with the students is that doing so creates a mechanism whereby students can discuss and come to own the learning intentions and success criteria, making it more likely that they will be able to apply the learning intentions and success criteria in the context of their own work.

Shirley Clarke (2005) gives the following example. A middle years teacher has been teaching a unit on food production in the developing world. She tells the class that the learning intention is to understand the impact of banana production on the banana producers themselves. The students study this topic, and at the end of the unit, the teacher conducts an end-of-unit assessment, in which students are required to show what they have learned about the impact of banana production on banana producers. Since they have been spending an hour a day on this topic for the previous two weeks, most of the students are able to get high scores on the assessment. The problem with such an approach is that if we only test the students on the things we have taught them, they are, of course, likely to do well, but so what?

Clarke points out that this kind of shallow approach to teaching and assessment is often the result of confusion between the learning intention and the context of the learning. She suggests that in this particular example, a far better learning intention would be to understand the impact of production on producers in the developing world; banana production should be the context of the learning. The success criterion—how the teacher finds out whether the learning intention has been satisfied or not—could then be whether the students can transfer what they learned about banana production to, say, sugar production.

This highlights a profound but poorly understood point. As teachers, we are not interested in our students' ability to do what we have taught them to do. We are only interested in their ability to apply their newly acquired knowledge to a similar but different context.

This is perhaps clearest in mathematics. If a teacher teaches students to add fractions with a worked example, such as ¹/₂ + ³/₅, once she has done that, she is no longer interested in the students' ability to add ¹/₂ and ³/₅. The students can do that problem because they have just been shown it! What the teacher wants to know is whether the students can transfer their newly acquired knowledge to a reasonably similar but different pair of fractions. Likewise, if she teaches students how to find the area of a particular trapezoid, that individual problem is no longer interesting. What is important is whether the students can transfer their knowledge to other trapezoids.

In English, when we get students to correct punctuation on a final draft, we're looking beyond that piece of writing; we hope that students will transfer what they have learned to other pieces of writing.

This is why, as Alfie Kohn pointed out, scoring rubrics that are too detailed can be counterproductive. If you specify in detail what students are to achieve, then they may well achieve it, but that is probably all they will be able to do (Kohn, 2006). The clearer you are about what you want, the more likely you are to get it, but the less likely it is to mean anything.

Table 3.3 draws on the work of Clarke (2005) to provide some examples in which the learning intention is confused with the context of the learning and ways in which the learning objective might be reframed.

Another benefit of separating the learning intention from the context of the learning is that it makes it much easier to differentiate instruction without creating a classroom in which different students are working toward different goals. All students can be working toward the same learning intention; the differentiation comes in the success criteria. One particularly effective way to do this is to differentiate the success criteria by how far students are able to transfer their learning to novel contexts. All students should be able to transfer what they have learned to very similar contexts, while others can be challenged by assessing how far they can transfer what they have learned.

We have to be able to distinguish between the intended learning outcomes and the instructional activities that we hope will result in those outcomes, and this is a distinction that many teachers find hard to make.

Table 3.3: Examples of Confused and Clarified Learning Intentions

Confused Learning Objective	Clarified Learning Objective	Context of Learning
To be able to write instructions on how to change a bicycle tyre	To be able to write clear instructions	Changing a bicycle tyre
To be able to present an argument for or against assisted suicide	To be able to present an argument either for or against an emotionally charged proposition	Assisted suicide
To know what the local priest does	To know the duties and responsibilities of religious leaders	The local priest
To produce and analyse a questionnaire about movie-going habits	To construct and analyse questionnaire data	Movie-going habits
To design an experiment to find out what conditions pill bugs prefer	To design fair tests for scientific questions	Preferred habitat of pill bugs

I often ask teachers, "What are your learning intentions for this period?" Many times, teachers respond by saying things like, "I'm going to have the students . . ." and then specify an activity. When I follow up by asking what the teacher expects the students to learn as a result of the activity, I am often met with a blank stare, as if the question is meaningless or trivial. This is why good teaching is so extraordinarily difficult. It is relatively easy to think up cool stuff for students to do in classrooms, but the problem with such an activity-based approach is that too often, it is not clear what the students are going to learn. It is also relatively easy, on the other hand, to approach students directly about what you want them to learn, but this often results in unimaginative teaching. Teaching is hard, because as Grant Wiggins and Jay McTighe (2000) have pointed out, it has to be designed backward.

Issues in Constructing Learning Intentions

There are many sources of advice for teachers about the construction of learning intentions and success criteria—the works of Shirley Clarke in the UK and Rick Stiggins and his colleagues at the Assessment Training Institute in the US are particularly powerful in this regard—but the development of good learning intentions is more craft than science and will always depend on the creativity of teachers. Nevertheless, there are three issues in the development of learning intentions and success criteria that may be useful to think about:

1. Task-specific versus generic scoring rubrics

2. Product-focused versus process-focused criteria

3. Official versus student-friendly language

Task-Specific Versus Generic Scoring Rubrics

A scoring rubric—which is really just a way of presenting success criteria—can be task-specific, so that it applies to just a single task, or it can be generic, so that the same rubric can be applied to a number of different tasks (see Stiggins, 2001, pp. 314–322). Task-specific rubrics can be written in very clear language, so they are good for communicating accurately to students what is required for that particular task, but this strength is also a weakness in that they focus only on that specific task. This is the same issue that arose earlier in the discussion of contextualised learning intentions; by being specific about what we want, we focus the students' learning too much. Plus, students need to come to grips with a new rubric for each task. Judith Arter and Jay McTighe (2001) suggest that task-specific rubrics are generally more appropriate for summative assessment. When we want students to know exactly what we want them to show us they can do, then specific criteria are very useful. They make sure that students know what we are looking for, and thus they are useful at the end of learning. During learning, however, it is useful to build a degree of generality into scoring rubrics so as to promote transfer (for more on the characteristics of good rubrics, see Relearning by Design, 2000).

Product-Focused Versus Process-Focused Criteria

Most learning intentions and success criteria focus on the outcomes of learning, for example, by stating what students are expected to be able to do at the end of a period of instruction. This is very natural, because, as noted previously, the best learning needs to be designed backward from the intended destination. However, in the same way that during a car journey, it is helpful (and reassuring) to be informed that one is on the right track (for example, "You will pass a petrol station on the left"), process criteria can be useful, too. Clarke (2005) gives the following example:

> Learning intention: to write an effective characterisation
>
> Product success criterion: the reader will feel as if they know the person
>
> Process success criteria: the characterisation includes at least two of the following:
>
> - the character's hobbies and interests
> - the character's attitudes toward self and others
> - examples of the character's extrovert or introvert personality
> - examples of the character's likes and dislikes (p. 31)

Physical education teachers and athletics coaches are often very good at developing process criteria; they break complex skills down into simpler ones and then reassemble them. To those who have never had to teach throwing a ball, it just looks like one action, but coaches know that most children learn to do this better when it is broken down into a number of steps that are practised individually and then integrated into one fluid action.

Writing frames are also examples of process criteria, because they structure the student's response. However, in the same way that leg braces are useful to individuals with legs weakened by injury but are a constraint for those who are healthy, writing frames can help some students but will prevent others from responding creatively.

I vividly remember teaching a class of year nine students and assigning them the task of working out how many rectangles were produced by the intersection of a number of horizontal lines and a different number of vertical lines, as shown in the following figure.

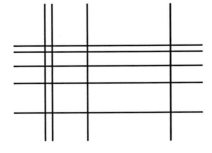

I had developed a set of process criteria that encouraged students to "try simpler cases" as recommended by George Polya (1945), for example, by looking at just two horizontal lines and then counting the rectangles formed by two, then three, then four vertical lines and so on. Within a matter of minutes, one of the students had written down the following mathematical formula:

$$\frac{m(m-1)}{2} \times \frac{n(n-1)}{2}$$

I asked to see his scratch work, and he said, "What scratch work?" He patiently pointed out to me that each rectangle was formed by a choice of a pair of horizontal lines and a choice of a pair of vertical lines. If there were m horizontal lines, then there were m choices for the first of the two horizontal lines and, therefore, $m - 1$ choices for the second horizontal line, giving a total of $m \times (m - 1)$ pairs in all. But then each pair of lines would get counted twice, so to get the number of choices of horizontal pairs, $m \times (m - 1)$ needed to be divided by 2. Applying a similar argument to the vertical lines and multiplying the two expressions together gave the solution.

For this student, my careful planning frame (had he paid any attention to it!) would have prevented him from finding a truly insightful solution that I had not seen. We need to realise that process criteria are, at the same time, both constraints *and* affordances for our students, and so we need to be thoughtful about how we frame them and how we use them.

Having said this, process criteria are particularly important in helping students become owners of their own learning (see chapter 7). If the teacher has spent some time helping students develop a "nose for quality" as described previously, then the students will be all too aware of the gap between where they are and where they want to be. What they will not know is how to move forward. Providing them with process criteria breaks up the long journey from where the learners are to where they need to be into smaller steps, making it more manageable.

When we are in summative mode, the purpose of success criteria is to determine the extent to which students have been successful. When we are in formative mode, the purpose of success criteria is to bring about that success.

Official Versus Student-Friendly Language

National standards are often written in rather formal language, and it is not particularly easy for students (or teachers!) to work out what they mean. As a result, some authors advocate that teachers should adapt the standards and present them to students in student-friendly language. There are merits in such an approach, but it is also worth remembering that the language used in national standards is often characteristic of the discipline that the standards represent. Students might not understand what the term *sense of audience* means, and one response might be to try to express the meaning in simpler words, but it is also important that students come to understand the phrase *sense of audience* as a term in English classes. Student-friendly language can be useful as students are introduced to a discipline, but it is also important to help students develop the habits of mind that define the discipline, and coming to terms with the "official" language is part of that process.

Practical Techniques

An important technique for helping students understand learning intentions and success criteria is asking them to look at samples of other students' work and to engage in a discussion about the strengths and weaknesses of each. For example, a middle years science teacher is teaching a class how to write laboratory reports. Before students are asked to write their own reports, he chooses five samples of work from one of last year's classes, and groups of students have to decide whether some of these are better than others. If they decide that some are, indeed, better than others (as they always do!), they rank the pieces of work in terms of their quality, and then each group reports back in a whole-class session. Once the responses from each group have been shared, the teacher invites students to give reasons for their views, and these are then used to co-construct a scoring rubric for laboratory reports. As noted previously, this is not a democratic process. The teacher uses his own subject knowledge to shape the discussion to ensure that the scoring rubric faithfully captures developing notions of competence in the subject.

To this end, it can be useful for the teacher to have prepared a model of progression that can be used to underpin a scoring rubric. For example, a group of geography educators proposed the following model of progression in geographical writing (Davies, Durbin, Clarke & Dale, 2004):

- **Stage 1** *Extremes:* using accurate place names to identify locations and using extremes like hard/soft, hilly/flat, wet/dry, rich/poor to describe features and places.

- **Stage 2** *Different types:* recognising different kinds of places using words like warm, cool, freezing and very hot as well as hot and cold; using terms like detached, semi-detached, terraced and flats to describe different dwellings.

- **Stage 3** *Comparisons:* using number to compare features (e.g. twice as many people, half the range of temperature) and places, and describing the differences within places.

- **Stage 4** *Ratios and patterns:* grouping descriptions to give a sense of a whole place and using terms that combine ideas such as population density, converge and diverge, and humidity to describe features and places. (p. 23)

While it would probably not be helpful to give the students a model such as this, it is helpful for teachers to have thought about models of progression in their subjects ahead of time.

Some teachers wonder why a class should spend time looking at other students' work when they could be doing their own work, but as many teachers have discovered, students are much better at spotting errors and weaknesses in the work of others than they are in their own. Once students have pointed out such errors or weaknesses, they are more likely to avoid repeating them in their own work. One way of drawing together a session in which the class determines weaknesses in other students' work is to compile a list of "What Not to Write" (based on the TV show *What Not to Wear*) in which students share pitfalls that they recommend others should avoid.

It can also be useful to use student samples to exemplify excellent work. A secondary school teacher had assigned a politics class the task of writing a paper on the system of checks and balances in the Constitution of Australia. The teacher collected the papers and assigned each paper a provisional mark in her markbook but did not write anything on the papers. The following day, students received their own essays, together with copies of what the teacher had judged to be the three best essays in the class, and were asked to read them before the next lesson. During the next lesson, the class discussed what they thought were the important features of the three essays judged as good. All students (including those who had written the three selected essays) were then invited to redraft and resubmit their essays. Two particular features of this technique are worth noting. First, it exemplifies excellent work in a concrete way. Second, and probably more important, the students whose essays are not selected have to do intellectual work to compare their own work with the samples provided, so the feedback is more engaging than it would be had the students been given feedback produced by someone else.

Students are able to engage with ideas of quality in work at a very young age. A kindergarten class was painting with watercolour paint, and after about fifteen minutes, the teacher held up one girl's painting and asked the class to suggest why the teacher thought this was a particularly good example of painting. A boy looked at the painting that was being held up and looked at his own painting, and after some moments, he said, "Because it's not all brown." The boy realised that he had been too impatient in his painting and had not waited for the paint to dry before using a different colour. Other techniques for engaging students at an early age include the "daily sign in" and a process called "choose-swap-choose".

In "daily sign in" each week, the teacher prepares a large sheet of paper with the students' names down the left-hand side of the sheet and columns headed with the days of the week. Each day, when the students arrive, they sign their names in the appropriate place. Obviously at this age, some students are able to write their names quite legibly, while others are placing little more than squiggles in the box. On Friday of each week, each student goes to the sign-in sheet with a peer, and they have to agree which of their five sign-ins is the best.

"Choose-swap-choose" works on a similar basis. For example, the teacher asks each student in the class to write the letter *d* ten times. Each student then chooses which of his ten *d*'s he thinks is the best and circles it. The students then swap with a neighbour, and the neighbour circles which of his peer's *d*'s he thinks is the best. If the neighbours disagree, they discuss why.

The opportunities for students to talk about quality work appear to be practically unlimited. A languages teacher wanted her students to understand what a good French accent sounded like, so she organised her class into groups of five students and gave each group a card with the same short passage of French. In each group, students took turns reading the passage aloud, and then, after all the students in the group had read the passage, the group had to decide which of them had the best French accent. The class then heard from each of the chosen group representatives, and the teacher led a whole-class discussion about the strengths and weaknesses of each of the accents the class had heard.

For older students (say, year four and up), one technique that is particularly useful both for getting students to clarify, share and understand learning intentions and for informing the teacher about the students' level of understanding is to have the students design test items, with correct answers, about what they have been learning. In a study involving several experiments with 260 university students, this was shown to be more effective than administering practice tests, giving students study guides or leaving them to prepare for tests in their own way.

In one of the study's experiments, students who created their own outlines of what they had been learning and then generated study questions based on these outlines outperformed students who had been given materials designed by others, but only on those items that assessed aspects of the course for which the students had generated items. The problem with this study is that it is not clear whether the increased achievement was due to the creation of an outline or the generation of study questions. A second experiment showed that it was the fact that students generated their own items that had the effect—students who generated their own items outperformed students given items generated by other students (Foos, Mora & Tkacz, 1994).

This can be a particularly effective strategy with disaffected older students, who often feel threatened by tests. Writing a test for the topic they have completed, and knowing that the teacher is going to mark the questions rather than the answers, can be a hugely liberating experience for many students.

The other benefit of having students generate their own questions is that the teacher can find out what the students think they have been learning. This is often different from what the teacher thinks they have been learning, but what the teacher thinks the students have been learning is irrelevant! A good illustration of this was an inquiry science lesson in which the teacher asked the students to design an experiment to find out what kind of habitat was preferred by pill bugs, specifically, whether they preferred dry or moist conditions and warm or cool conditions. At the end, the students were asked to devise a question that the teacher could use to find out whether the activity had been successful, and the vast majority of students wrote questions that asked what kind of habitat was preferred by pill bugs. This showed the teacher that the point of the activity—that of devising a fair test of a scientific question or proposition—had been largely missed by the students, no doubt in part because of the way the teacher had framed the learning intentions (see table 3.3, page 61).

Of course, there will be times when it is appropriate simply to present the learning intentions and success criteria to the students. With younger students, many teachers have found the acronyms WALT (We are learning to) and WILF (What I'm looking for) to be useful ways of getting students started with learning intentions and success criteria. These can also be supplemented with TIB (This is because) to help students see how a particular learning intention fits in with other things they have done.

Conclusion

It seems obvious that to get anywhere, it helps to be clear about where you are going, and yet, until relatively recently, sharing learning intentions and success criteria with students has not been regarded as important. Unfortunately, in many regions, the pendulum has swung too far the other way: a lesson is regarded as a bad lesson if the teacher fails to post a learning objective at the start.

This chapter has reviewed research evidence that shows it is important that students know where they are going in their learning and what counts as quality work, but there cannot be any simple formula for doing this. Like everything else in teaching, there are no simple rules, and it is up to the teacher to exercise professional judgment in how best to communicate learning intentions and success criteria to students. While there cannot be any simple formula, there are a number of practical techniques that many teachers have found useful, some of which have been summarised in this chapter.

Once teachers and students are clear about where they are headed, the next step, of course, is to understand whether they are on track, and for that, it is necessary to collect evidence about where students are in their learning, which is the subject of the next chapter.

CHAPTER 4

Eliciting Evidence of Learners' Achievement

We discovered in chapter 3 the importance of being clear about what we want students to learn. Once we've accomplished that, we need to ascertain where the students are in their learning. In many classrooms, the process of eliciting such evidence is done mainly on the fly—teachers almost always plan the instructional activities in which they will engage their students, but they rarely plan in detail how they are going to find out where the students are in their learning. This chapter emphasises the importance of planning this process and provides guidelines on what makes a good question, as well as some alternatives to questions. The chapter also offers some practical guidance on how to use questions effectively to adjust instruction to meet students' needs.

Finding Out What Students Know

The following are two questions used in the Third International Mathematics and Science Study (TIMSS; quoted by Vinner, 1997):

Question 1
Which fraction is the smallest?

A. $\frac{1}{6}$ B. $\frac{2}{3}$

C. $\frac{1}{3}$ D. $\frac{1}{2}$

Question 2
Which fraction is the largest?

A. $\frac{4}{5}$ B. $\frac{3}{4}$

C. $\frac{5}{8}$ D. $\frac{7}{10}$

These two items appear to be quite similar, although the second question is obviously somewhat more complex because of the larger numbers involved. However, the second question turns out to be *much* more difficult than the first. For middle years students in Israel, for example, the success rate on the first item was 88 per cent but for the second, only 46 per cent (Vinner, 1997). In other words, only about half of the students who answered the first question correctly could also answer the second.

When I ask teachers why this might be, a number of possible reasons emerge. Some suggest that the first item is easier than the second because the fractions in the first question can be easily visualised. Others suggest that apart from option B, which is obviously bigger than C, they are all unitary fractions (fractions with a numerator of 1), which makes comparison easier. A third common suggestion is that the lowest common multiple is already present in the first question but not in the second and so has to be calculated, making this a two-step problem, which is obviously more complicated—although it is interesting to note that many adults (including maths teachers!) prefer to answer the second question by converting each fraction to a percentage rather than by using the method that students are typically taught in the middle years.

All of these explanations are credible, but a little more detective work reveals something rather interesting. In answering the second question, 39 per cent of the students chose B. Since this question was answered correctly by 46 per cent of the students, it was answered incorrectly by 54 per cent, but 39 per cent chose the *same* incorrect answer. In other words, almost three-fourths of the students who answered incorrectly chose the *same* incorrect answer.

This is highly significant. After all, if students' errors were random, then we would expect each of the incorrect answers to be chosen as often as the other incorrect responses, so that approximately 18 percent of students would choose each of B, C and D. Instead, option B was chosen more than twice as often as the other two incorrect responses combined. This suggests that students' errors on this item are not random but systematic.

The most plausible explanation is that the choice of option B is related to how students learn about fractions. Although confusing at first, children come to realise that one-fifth is less than one-fourth because the whole has been divided into more pieces. From this, many students conclude that the largest fraction is the one with the smallest denominator, and the smallest fraction is the one with the largest denominator. This rule works perfectly well for unitary fractions but does not work in general.

When attempting the first question, a student with this incomplete understanding of fractions will simply look for the largest denominator, find 6, and choose A—the correct answer. However, the same strategy applied to the second question leads the student to look for the smallest denominator, find 4, and choose B—an incorrect answer.

While we cannot be sure that this is the only reason for the differences in responses for the two questions, it is significant that adding the percentage of students who chose the correct answer to the second question (46 per cent) to that of those who chose the answer generated by the naïve strategy (39 per cent) gives us 85 per cent, which is very close to the 88 per cent correct figure for the first question. In other words, there is strong evidence that many students who got the first question right got it right for the wrong reason.

Why does this matter? Because when we, as teachers, ask students a question, and we get the answer we were hoping for, we tend to conclude that the students' learning is heading in the right direction. If, however, our questions are more like the first question than the second question, then there is a real danger that we will assume that our students' learning is on track when it is, in fact, heading off in a completely different direction.

Where Do Students' Ideas Come From?

Many students, when asked to describe the following shape, say it's an "upside-down triangle".

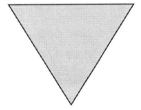

It is common to regard this as a misconception since it appears that the students do not realise that shape and orientation are independent of each other; a triangle remains a triangle no matter which way it is oriented. However, some students describe this shape as an upside-down triangle even though they know that the orientation does not matter for the naming of the shape, because they are using vernacular, rather than mathematical, language.

A good example of this distinction is the word *square*. In the mathematics classroom, this word means a quadrilateral with four equal sides and four equal angles. In the world outside the mathematics classroom, however, the word *square* is often used to describe orientation rather than shape (for example, a picture can be "square" on a wall even when its sides are not the same length), and shapes that are, in fact, squares are described in ways based on their orientation rather than their shape (a baseball "diamond" is, after all, a square).

What seems like a misconception is often, and perhaps usually, a perfectly good conception in the wrong place. Describing a triangle as inverted is obviously an error in the mathematics classroom but a helpful aid to communication in other contexts (try Googling the phrase "inverted triangle" to see what I mean).

The same is true in other school subjects. When a child says, "I spended all my money," this could be regarded as a misconception, but it makes more sense to regard this as overuse of a general rule. Adding *d* or *ed* to a verb to form the past tense works most of the time, so the child may be guilty of nothing more than playing the odds!

Some people have argued that these unintended conceptions are the result of poor teaching. If only the teacher had phrased his explanation more carefully, had ensured that no unintended features were learned alongside the intended features, then these misconceptions would not arise. But this argument fails to acknowledge two important points. The first is that this kind of overgeneralisation is a fundamental feature of human thinking. A child might initially associate the term *panda* with a particular fluffy toy but then will realise that other things are called *panda*, too. Pretty soon, the word *panda* becomes associated with a range of fluffy toys, some of which are not pandas, until the child learns to discriminate between pandas, giraffes and lions.

The key insight here is that children are active in the construction of their own knowledge. They literally "make sense" of the things that go on around them, including what we teach, and sometimes, the sense they make is not what we intended. Perhaps the best example of this is the answer you get when you ask children between the ages of four and seven, "What causes the wind?" "God", which is what most adults assume children will say, is a common response, but an equally popular answer is "trees". This is not likely to be something that they have been taught and misremembered. Children have observed that trees sway when the wind blows and have concluded that a correlation implies causation.

The second point is that even if we wanted to, we are unable to control the students' environments to the extent necessary for unintended conceptions not to arise. For example, many students believe that the result of multiplying 2.3 by 10 is 2.30. It is highly unlikely that they have been taught this. Rather, this belief arises as a result of observing regularities in what they see around them. They see that $7 \times 10 = 70$, $8 \times 10 = 80$, and so on, so they conclude that the result of multiplying whole numbers by ten is just to add a zero. We could make such a "misconception" less likely to arise by introducing decimals before teaching multiplying single-digit numbers by ten, but that would be ridiculous.

Teachers must acknowledge that what their students learn is not necessarily what they intended, and this is inevitable because of the unpredictability of teaching. Thus, it is essential that teachers explore students' thinking before assuming that students have understood something. However, generating questions that provide these powerful insights into students' thinking is far from straightforward.

Consider the following pair of equations:

$$3a = 24$$
$$a + b = 16$$

When asked what a and b are, many students respond that the equations can't be solved. The teacher might conclude that they need some more help with equations of this sort, but often, the reason behind the difficulties with this item is not the students' mathematical skills but their *beliefs* (Schoenfeld, 1989). When students are encouraged to talk about their difficulty, they often say things like, "I keep on getting b is eight, but it can't be because a is." The reason that many students have developed such a belief is that before they were introduced to solving equations, they practised substituting numbers into algebraic formulas, where each letter represented a different number. Although the students were not taught that each letter must represent a unique number, they have generalised implicit rules from their previous experience; they talk of "upside-down triangles" because we always show them triangles where the lowest side is horizontal and then compound the error when we teach them that the area of a triangle is half the base multiplied by the height (if there is no "right way up", how can a triangle have a base?).

The point here is that had the sixteen in the second equation been any other number at all, provided they had the necessary arithmetical skills, students would have solved these equations, and the teacher would, in all likelihood, assume that the class's learning was on track.

Questions that give us insight into student learning are not easy to generate and often do not look like traditional test questions. Indeed, to some teachers, they appear unfair. That is certainly the reaction of many maths teachers to the following question, taken from the Chelsea Diagnostic Test for Algebra (Hart, Brown, Kerslake, Küchemann & Ruddock, 1985):

Simplify (if possible): 2*a* + 5*b*

The question is perceived as unfair because students "know" that in answering test questions, you have to do some work, so it must be possible to simplify this expression; otherwise, the teacher wouldn't have asked the question—after all, you don't get points in a test for doing nothing. Such a question may well fall short of standards and fairness guidelines established for items in a high-stakes test (for example, Educational Testing Service, 2002). But for finding out whether students understand a key principle in algebra, it is a useful question. If a student can be tempted to simplify $2a + 5b$, then the teacher should want to know that, because addressing this misunderstanding will be essential before the student can make progress in algebra.

Similar issues are raised by asking students which of the following two fractions is the larger:

$$\tfrac{3}{7} \text{ or } \tfrac{3}{11}$$

This item is generally not answered correctly by middle years students. It is seen by many teachers as a trick question and for that reason probably should not be used in a high-stakes test. But it is a very good question for generating classroom discussion. The fact that this item is seen as a trick question shows how deeply ingrained into our practice is the idea that assessment should allow us to sort, rank and mark students, rather than inform the teacher what needs to be done next.

In another example, a teacher was conducting a lesson about the molecular structure of matter. She had explained to students that water was composed of molecules, each of which had two atoms of hydrogen linked to an atom of oxygen, and asked the students to draw a sketch of what this might look like. The students in the class produced appropriate sketches, but when the teacher asked the class what was between the molecules, every single student said "water"—the students thought that the molecules were *in* the water, not that they *were* the water.

Whether to go over something one more time or to move on is a professional decision that the teacher must make, and in doing so, she needs to take a number of factors into account. For example, some aspects of the curriculum may be important but not consequential in terms of learning progressions. In other words, if a student fails to learn something at that point, he can still make progress. On the other hand, some things are absolute prerequisites for any meaningful progress. For example, there is no point trying to teach adding fractions if students are not able to generate equivalent fractions for a given fraction. It is also necessary to take into account the wider context. For example, a score of four or five on one of the College Board's Advanced Placement examinations confers university credit, whereas scores of one, two and three do not. So a teacher might judge that moving on at a particular point is the right thing to do even though many students have not understood something, on the grounds that for a student, getting a four rather than a three represents a real difference, whereas getting a two rather than a one does not. I am not saying that this is right or wrong. It is a professional decision that each teacher needs to make for herself. What is unprofessional is to make that decision without finding out what the students in the class know. Questions that provide a window into students' thinking are not easy to generate, but they are crucially important if we are to improve the quality of students' learning.

One common objection at this point is that teachers do not have time to develop such questions, not least because they are too busy marking, but this just shows how ineffective many of our standard classroom routines are. Every teacher has had the experience of writing the same thing on fifteen or twenty students' notebooks because the students were allowed to leave the classroom before the teacher discovered that the students had failed to understand some crucial point. So the important issue is this: does the teacher find out whether students have understood something when they are still in the class, when there is time to do something about it, or does the teacher only discover this once he looks at the students' notebooks? Viewed from this perspective, marking can be seen as the punishment given to teachers for failing to find out that they did not achieve the intended learning when the students were in front of them. Does the teacher get the class's learning back on track with the class in front of him, in one go, and when the meanings of students' responses and the teacher's questions can be negotiated, or does the teacher do it one student at a time, after they have gone away, and in writing?

There is no doubt that in the United States, most teachers spend a majority of their lesson preparation time marking student work, and almost invariably doing so alone. In other countries, much, if not the majority, of lesson preparation time is spent planning how new topics can be introduced and which contexts and examples will be used, and teachers work in groups to devise questions to find out whether their teaching has been successful. As noted previously, questions that give us this window into students' thinking are hard to generate, and teacher collaboration will help to build a stock of good questions.

Practical Techniques

Teacher-led classroom discussion is one of the most universal instructional practices. Typically, this follows a model termed "initiation-response-evaluation" (I-R-E) by researchers (for example, Mehan, 1979): the teacher asks a question, selects a student to answer the question, and then responds to the student's answer, generally with some kind of evaluation of what the student said.

Obviously, teacher talk dominates such interactions, but there are significant differences among countries in the relative proportions of teacher and student talk. American teachers seem to talk *less* than teachers in countries with higher average levels of achievement. For example, the 1999 TIMSS video study found that in US middle years mathematics classrooms there were eight teacher words for every student word. In Japan and Hong Kong, the figures were thirteen and sixteen, respectively (Hiebert et al., 2003). So although many people assume that American teachers talk too much, they actually talk less than teachers in countries with higher performance. It would appear that how much students learn depends more on the quality than the quantity of talk.

As part of a larger study of primary school classrooms, Ted Wragg and his colleagues analysed one thousand teacher questions they had recorded. Over half the questions (57 per cent) were managerial questions, such as "Who has finished all the questions?" or "Have you got your books?" Another one-third of the questions required only recall of previously provided information, such as, "How many legs does an insect have?" Only 8 per cent of the questions asked by teachers required the students to analyse, to make inferences or to generalise, such as, "Why is a bird not an insect?" (Brown & Wragg, 1993). Less than 10 per cent of the questions that were asked by teachers in these classrooms actually caused any new learning. The others were rehearsing things the students already knew or were about classroom management. Addressing this seems like an obvious way to improve student learning.

I suggest there are only two good reasons to ask questions in class: to cause thinking and to provide information for the teacher about what to do next. As an example of the former, a year six teacher had asked a class whether a triangle could have two right angles, and students were discussing their answers in groups. In one group, one student believed that he could, by building a really long, thin triangle, because he had remembered being told by someone that parallel lines meet at infinity. Another student in the group knew that the three angles had to add up to 180° and realised that by having two right angles, he had already reached that total, and so he wondered whether it was possible to have an angle of 0°. A girl in the group was confident that she could create a triangle with three right angles, if she was allowed to place one corner at the North Pole and the other two on the equator (which the first two students dismissed, saying that it wasn't a proper triangle). Although this question looks like a closed question, answering it was a valuable activity for these students because it caused thinking.

The other reason to ask questions is to collect information to inform teaching, for example, when a science teacher asks a class, "Which way does light travel? From my eye to the object or from the object to my eye?" This, too, is a closed question. After all, there are two answers, and one is incorrect. But it is a valuable question to ask, because many students believe that light travels from the eye to the object being seen, rather than the other way around.

Another finding of the TIMSS video studies, which confirmed findings of earlier studies (for example, Weiss, Pasley, Smith, Banilower & Heck, 2003; Rowan, Harrison & Hayes, 2004) was that American classrooms were characterised by relatively low degrees of student engagement. Understanding why this is so significant requires a brief detour into some recent work on the development of human abilities.

Student Engagement

In his book *Outliers*, Malcolm Gladwell (2008b) presents data on the twenty-five members of a Junior Hockey League team in Canada called the Medicine Hat Tigers, including height, weight, date of birth, position and so on. He then invites the reader to look at the data for unusual features. The remarkable feature of the data, which few people notice until it is pointed out to them, is that eight of the twenty-five players were born in January and another six were born in February or March. The leagues are organised by age group, with those born in the same calendar year playing together. When children begin to play hockey in competitive leagues, those born in the early part of the year are a little stronger, faster and bigger than the rest, and so they are more likely to get picked for the team. As a result, they get more time on the ice and are also likely to get more coaching. Over time, this builds up into a significant advantage.

The same effects have been noticed in other sports, too—those born soonest after the date used to divide age groups are more likely to be playing at the highest levels. It has been termed the "Matthew effect" (Stanovich, 1986): "For to all those who have, more will be given, and they will have an abundance; but from those who have nothing, even what they have will be taken away" (Matt. 25:29, New Revised Standard Version). Why does this matter? Because we create exactly the same kind of effect in our classrooms every day.

In almost any classroom, some students nearly dislocate their shoulders in their eagerness to show the teacher that they have an answer to the question that the teacher has just asked. In the same classroom, however, other students try to stay below the radar and avoid being called on. One teacher described his classroom thus:

> I'd become dissatisfied with the closed Q&A style that my unthinking teaching had fallen into, and I would frequently be lazy in my acceptance of right answers and sometimes even tacit complicity with a class to make sure none of us had to work too hard . . . They and I knew that if the Q&A wasn't going smoothly, I'd change the question, answer it myself or only seek answers from the "brighter students". There must have been times (still are?) where an outside observer would see my lessons as a small discussion group surrounded by many sleepy onlookers. (Black et al., 2004, p. 11)

High-engagement classroom environments appear to have a significant impact on student achievement. In one study, 191 students in seven year four classrooms followed the Thinking Together program (Dawes, Mercer & Wegerif, 2000) in which teachers were provided with twelve lesson plans that were designed to help students develop their ability to use language as a tool for thinking about science and mathematics, both individually and in collaboration with other students. The researchers found that these students outperformed controls in similar schools on both teacher-constructed measures and standardised science achievement tests (Mercer, Dawes, Wegerif & Sams, 2004). More surprisingly, these students outperformed controls on Raven's Progressive Matrices, which is a purely spatial test of intelligence. Engaging in classroom discussion really does make you smarter.

So, when teachers allow students to choose whether to participate or not—for example, by allowing them to raise their hands to show they have an answer—they are actually making the achievement gap worse, because those who are participating are getting smarter, while those avoiding engagement are forgoing the opportunities to increase their ability.

This is why many teachers now employ a rule of "no hands up except to *ask* a question" in their classrooms (Leahy, Lyon, Thompson & Wiliam, 2005). The teacher poses a question and then picks on a student at random. One middle years teacher describes this technique as "pose-pause-pounce-bounce". She poses the question, pauses for at least five seconds (sometimes, to help her measure the time, she mutters, under her breath, "One, two, three, four, got to wait a little more"), pounces on one student at random for the answer, and then bounces that student's answer to another student, again at random, saying, "What do you think of that answer?"

Some teachers claim to be able to choose students at random without any help, but most teachers realise that when they are in a hurry to wrap up a discussion so that the class can move on, they are often drawn to one of the usual suspects for a good answer. This is why many teachers have found the use of some randomisation device useful. Examples of these can be downloaded from the Internet, and randomisation routines are often included in the software supplied with interactive whiteboards. There are now even apps for the iPhone into which student names can be entered and then drawn at random. However, a beaker of icy pole sticks (or for science teachers, tongue depressors) on which the students' names are written does the job just as well. The icy pole sticks are also much more flexible; one teacher has punished inattentive students by writing their name on ten additional sticks and adding them to the beaker. If there is any concern that the teacher is rigging the choice of sticks, many teachers resolve the issue by giving the beaker of sticks to a student to be the "selector" for the day.

The major advantage of icy pole sticks can also be a disadvantage. It is essential to replace the sticks to ensure that students who have recently answered know they need to stay on task, but then the teacher cannot guarantee that all students will get a turn to answer. One way around this is to leave the selected sticks out of the beaker but then replace them when students who have already answered a question seem off task.

Selecting students at random is a radical change in the "classroom contract" (Brousseau, 1984) and will not be welcomed by many students who are accustomed to classrooms where participation is optional. Most teachers realise that being called upon at random will be a shock for students unused to participation in classrooms. However, moving to random selection can also be unpopular with students who participate regularly. For some, this is because they are no longer able to show the teacher that they have an answer. One way to tackle this issue is to ask two students at random for responses to a question, but for the third answer, ask the remainder of the class if anyone has anything else to contribute. It is also essential to ask the question first and then pick the student or students to answer. Doing it the other way around guarantees that all but the selected student know they need not pay attention.

For other students, random questioning is unwelcome because they are unable to control when they are asked questions. In one classroom, three students who were perceived by their teachers as having their hands up in response to every question actually removed their icy pole sticks from the beaker when the teacher wasn't looking. When this was discovered, they revealed that they only raised their hands when they had an answer, which was most of the time. However, they found the prospect of being asked to respond when they did not have an answer threatening to their image of themselves as high-performing students, and this feeling was so strong that they preferred never answering questions to the risk of being asked a question to which they did not know the answer (Barry & Hardy, 2010).

When teachers do call on students at random—what Doug Lemov (2010) terms *cold calling*—many students will still resist engagement by responding with, "I don't know." How the teacher responds to this is crucial. Some teachers accept this and move on to ask the same question of another student, but this, in effect, allows the student to opt out. By adopting a rule of "no hands up except to ask a question", the teacher has implied that the classroom should be one in which all students are engaged. However, the student has indicated that she does not wish to engage, and the teacher has, in turn, accepted this. In other words, the student has successfully resisted the teacher's attempt to change the classroom contract. A better response is for the teacher to say, "OK; I'll come back to you," and then go around the classroom and get a number of responses to the question, after which the teacher comes back to the original student and says, "Now, which of those answers do you like best?" Even when the other students have answered with a single correct response, it is still valuable to go back to the original student simply to get her to repeat the correct response, because it emphasises that this is a classroom in which there are no opt-outs (Lemov, 2010).

Often, students will say, "I don't know," not because they do not know, but because they cannot be bothered to think. Henry Ford once said that we know thinking is difficult because of the lengths people go to in order to avoid doing it. Although the teacher first needs to be sure that this *is* the reason for the student's response, in such situations, Ellin Keene suggests that teachers ask, "OK, but if you did know, what would you say?"

Other possibilities that support the students without letting them off the hook are allowing students to "phone a friend", or for multiple-choice items, they can "ask the audience" or ask to go "fifty-fifty", where two incorrect responses are removed. All these strategies derive their power from the fact that classroom participation is not optional, and even when the student resists, the teacher looks for ways to maintain the student's engagement.

Wait Time

How much time a teacher allows a student to respond before evaluating the response is also important. Teachers do not allow students much time to answer questions (Rowe, 1974), and if they do not receive a response quickly, they will often "help" the student by providing a clue, weakening the question in some way, or moving on to another student. However, the amount of time between the student's answer and the teacher's evaluation of that answer is just as, if not more, important. Of course, when the question is a simple matter of factual recall, then allowing a student time to reflect and expand upon the answer is unlikely to help much. If you don't know the capital of the Northern Territory, extra time isn't going to help. But when the question requires thought, increasing the time between the end of the student's answer and the teacher's evaluation from the average wait time of less than a second to three seconds produces measurable increases in learning, although according to Kenneth Tobin (1987), increases beyond three seconds have little effect and may cause lessons to lose pace.

Alternatives to Questions

Asking questions may not be the best way to generate good class-room discussions. Asking a class which country was most to blame for the outbreak of World War I invites students to plump for one country or another. If, instead, the teacher makes a statement, such as, "Russia was most to blame for the outbreak of World War I," students seem to respond more thoughtfully because they realise that just agreeing or dissenting is not enough—reasons have to be given (Dillon, 1988). Similarly, asking, "Are all squares rectangles?" is likely to yield a less-thoughtful discussion than framing what is, in effect, exactly the same question as a statement: "All squares are rectangles."

The quality of discussion is usually enhanced further when students are given the opportunity to discuss their responses in pairs or small groups before responding (a technique often called "think-pair-share").

Evaluative and Interpretive Listening

John Wooden was one of the greatest college basketball coaches of all time—some have suggested that he was the greatest coach of any sport (Serwer, 2010). He was once asked why other coaches were not as successful, and he said, "They don't listen. Listening is the best way to learn. You have to listen to those who you are supervising" (Serwer, 2010). But of course, what matters is *how* you listen.

When teachers listen to student responses, many focus more on the correctness of the answers than what they can learn about the student's understanding (Even & Tirosh, 1995; Heid, Blume, Zbiek & Edwards, 1999). It is easy to identify such teachers because when they get incorrect answers from students, they respond by saying things like, "Almost," "Close," or "Nearly; try again." What the teacher is really saying is, "Give me the correct answer so that I can get on with the rest of my script for the lesson." Brent Davis (1997) called such teacher behaviour "evaluative listening".

Teachers who listen evaluatively to their students' answers learn only whether their students know what they want them to know. If the students cannot answer correctly, then the teachers learn only that the students didn't get it and that they need to teach the material again, only, presumably, better. However, when teachers realise that there is often information about *how* to teach something better in what students say—and thus how to adjust the instruction to better meet students' needs—they listen *interpretively*. What such teachers seek to learn from the students' responses is not, "Did they get it?" but rather, "What can I learn about the students' thinking by attending carefully to what they say?" The shift from evaluative to interpretive listening was perhaps most eloquently summarised by a girl in a year seven classroom, who, when asked if she had noticed any change in her teacher over recent months, said, "When Miss used to ask a question, she used to be interested in the right answer. Now she's interested in what we think" (Hodgen & Wiliam, 2006, p. 16).

Question Shells

There are a number of general structures that can help frame questions in ways that are more likely to reveal students' thinking. One is the general structure of "Why is _____ an example of _____ ?" We saw one of these earlier ("Why is a bird not an insect?"). Similarly, rather than asking, "Is magnesium a metal?" more thoughtful and reasoned responses are likely to be generated by asking, "Why is magnesium a metal?" Other examples are shown in table 4.1.

Table 4.1: Examples of the Use of Question Shells

Original	Reframed
Is a square a trapezoid?	Why is a square a trapezoid?
Is carbon a metal?	Why is carbon not a metal?
Is *etre* a regular verb?	Why is *etre* an irregular verb?
Is this a sentence or a clause?	Why is this a clause rather than a sentence?
Is slate a metamorphic rock?	Why is slate a metamorphic rock?
Is *The Merchant of Venice* a comedy [or a tragedy]?	Why is *The Merchant of Venice* a comedy [or a tragedy]?
Is 23 prime?	Why is 23 prime?
Is photosynthesis an endothermic reaction?	Why is photosynthesis an endothermic reaction?

Another technique is to present students with a contrast and then ask them to explain the contrast, as shown in table 4.2.

Table 4.2: Examples of Questions Reframed in Terms of Contrasts

Original	Reframed
What is a prime number?	Why is 17 prime and 15 not?
What was life under apartheid like?	How were the lives of blacks and whites different under apartheid?
Is a bat a mammal?	Why is a bat a mammal and a penguin not?

Hot-Seat Questioning

Another useful technique for deepening classroom discussion is "hot-seat questioning". In the typical classroom, the teacher scatters questions around the class, which can create student engagement but tends to lead to a rather flat discussion in which there is little development of the subject matter. In hot-seat questioning, the teacher asks a student a question and then a series of follow-up questions to probe the student's ideas in depth. Other students in the class pay close attention because they know that at any minute, the teacher can turn from the student in the hot seat to anyone else in the class (chosen with a icy pole stick!) and say, "OK, summarise for me what James just said."

All these techniques are very effective ways of creating classroom engagement, but they are not necessarily good sources of evidence for teachers' instructional decision making. Probably the most common instructional decision made by teachers every day is, "Do I need to go over this one more time, or is it OK to move on?" In most classrooms, teachers generate the evidence for this decision by making up a question on the spur of the moment, asking the class, and selecting one of the students who raise their hands to answer. If that student answers correctly, the teacher generally says, "Good," and moves on. Asking a random student rather than a volunteer would be better, but the real problem is that the teacher is making a decision about the readiness of the whole class on the basis of the performance of one or two students. If teachers are to harness the power of high-quality questioning to inform their instructional decisions, they need to use all-student response systems routinely.

All-Student Response Systems

The idea of an all-student response system is very simple: the teacher asks a question in such a way that allows him to get a response from every student in real time. Some teachers employ class polls—going around the class and asking each student for his or her view on a question, such as, "Global warming: natural or anthropogenic?" or, "Macbeth: mad or bad?" but these work well only when every student expresses a view, and getting around the whole class can cause a considerable loss of momentum. It is best to collect the information from every student at the same time.

Techniques for All-Student Response

Many teachers collect information from the whole class simultaneously with techniques like "thinking thumbs" or "fist to five," where students indicate their confidence in their understanding either by the position of the thumb (pointing up: confident; horizontally: not sure; down: still confused) or with a number from zero to five by holding up a clenched fist (zero) or the appropriate number of fingers. The problem with such techniques is that they are self-reports, and, as we know from literally thousands of research studies, self-reports are unreliable.

However, a very small change can transform useless self-reports into a very powerful tool. Simply make sure that the question being asked is cognitive rather than affective—in other words, that it is asking about thinking, not a feeling. For example, a primary school teacher was teaching her students when the word *its* needed an apostrophe and when it didn't. On the board, she wrote the sentence, "Its on its way" and invited students to come up to the board and add any necessary punctuation. One student came up and added a full stop; a second added an apostrophe to the first *its*; and a third student added an apostrophe to the second *its*. The teacher then asked, "Is that now correct?" and every student had to respond by holding out a thumb pointing up or down. Just this small change in the way the question is posed creates a situation in which there is no place to hide for the students. If they signal that it is correct when it is not, then they reveal that they do not understand. On the other hand, if they signal that it is incorrect, then the teacher is likely to ask them to go to the front of the class to correct the error.

The same basic idea can be used in every school subject. In a secondary school chemistry class, for example, students were learning how to balance chemical equations. On the board, the teacher wrote the basic unbalanced equation for the reaction of mercury hydroxide with phosphoric acid to produce mercury phosphate and water:

$$Hg(OH)_2 + H_3PO_4 = Hg_3(PO_4)_2 + H_2O$$

Students were invited to go up to the board to suggest changes to help balance the equation, and after there were no more volunteers, the teacher asked the students to indicate, by thumbs up or down, whether the equation was now balanced.

In a primary school maths class, the teacher wanted to check on students' understanding of length and asked the students to indicate, by holding up one, two or three fingers, which of the statements were true of the lines shown in the following problem.

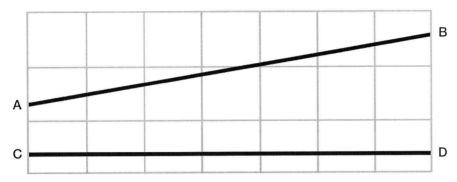

Which of the following statements is true?

1. AB is longer than CD.
2. AB is shorter than CD.
3. AB and CD are the same length.

A middle years science teacher had been teaching students to distinguish between different kinds of levers. After explaining that the key principle of the classification of levers concerns the relative arrangement of the load, the effort and the fulcrum, she illustrated the principle with three examples: a seesaw (type 1), a wheelbarrow (type 2) and a deep-sea fishing rod (type 3). To check the students' understanding, she asked the class how a pair of tweezers would be classified, requesting that each student hold up one, two or three fingers to indicate his or her response. She was surprised when most of the students indicated that they thought the tweezers were a type 2 lever. When she asked them why, the students replied that there were two arms to the tweezers. She realised that she needed to get the students to understand that it is the relative distribution of the effort, load and fulcrum that is important, not the number of components, by introducing more examples, such as a pair of scissors and a nutcracker.

In each of these four examples, the teacher was able to ensure both student engagement—after all, it is very easy to tell if a student has not voted—and high-quality evidence to help decide what to do next. The problem with using fingers and thumbs is that they work best with questions for which a single response is required (a drawback of most electronic clickers, too). That is why many teachers have adopted ABCD cards.

ABCD Cards

Each student has a number of cards, each of which bears a single letter. Some teachers just use A, B, C and D, while others use sets with nine cards: A, B, C, D, E, F, G, H and T (for true/false questions). These can be used just like fingers, but they also can be used with questions for which there is more than one correct answer, as in the following problem.

In which of the following diagrams is one-fourth of the area shaded?

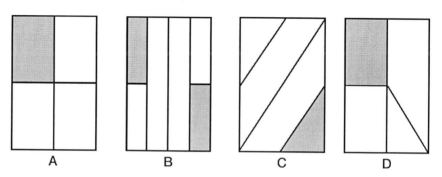

Most students should recognise that A and B represent one-fourth, and hopefully, most students will also realise that in diagram C, the fraction shaded is not one-fourth. Many teachers tell students that if one out of four regions in a diagram is shaded, the four regions have to have the same area for this to represent one-fourth, and as a result, many students come to believe that the fraction shaded in D is not one-fourth, because the regions are not the same area.

The use of multiple correct answers allows the teacher to incorporate items that support differentiation, by including some responses that all students should be able to identify correctly but also others that only the ablest students will be able to answer correctly. Such differentiation also helps keep the highest-achieving students challenged and, therefore, engaged.

ABCD cards can also be used when there are no right and wrong answers but different views. A teacher was discussing with a class the Heysel Stadium disaster of 1985, during which thirty-nine people died and over six hundred people were injured in rioting before a soccer game between Liverpool and Juventus. To help organise the discussion of this emotive issue, the teacher asked the students to indicate who they thought was most to blame:

A. The Liverpool fans

B. The Juventus fans

C. The police

D. The match organisers

E. The builders of the stadium

During the discussion, students displayed the cards indicating their views on their desks, and the teacher brought them in to the discussion at the appropriate time (students who changed their minds during the discussion were encouraged to change the letters they were displaying). At the end of the discussion, the teacher asked the students to vote again, and she was pleased to see that the class now had a much more complex view of the tragedy, with all of them displaying at least two cards.

One primary school teacher takes the idea of cards one step further with what she calls "letter corners". She uses multiple-choice questions with four options (A, B, C and D), and if each option has at least three students supporting it, she sends the students to the four corners of the room, which she has labelled A, B, C and D. The task of the students in each corner is to work out how to convince the students in the other corners that their choice is the best. Occasionally, students sneak from one corner to another. They move surreptitiously because they worry that the teacher will think that they are cheating, whereas, of course, the teacher celebrates such changes of mind as indicating that the students have learned something through discussion with peers.

ABCD cards can also be used to bridge two lessons. A middle years maths class was learning to solve equations with a single unknown, and five minutes before the end of the lesson, the teacher asked the students to work out the answers to six questions. Four of the questions related to what the class had done that lesson. As the students held up cards indicating their responses to these questions, the teacher was pleased to see that most of the students answered correctly. The last two questions related to what she planned to do for the following lesson, where the unknown quantity appeared on both sides of the equation. Very few students answered either of these two questions correctly, so she could see that what she had planned to do for the next lesson was, in fact, appropriate.

A major difficulty with ABCD cards is that they generally require teachers to have planned questions carefully ahead of time, and so they are less useful for spontaneous discussion, which is where mini whiteboards come in.

Mini Whiteboards

The mini whiteboard is sometimes touted as a modern invention but is really just the latest reincarnation of the slates used in 19th century classrooms. Whiteboards are powerful tools in that the teacher can quickly frame a question and get an answer from the whole class, whether asking primary school students to write down a four-letter word with a short "i" sound or, as we saw in chapter 2, asking students in an AP calculus class to sketch the graph of

$$y = \frac{1}{(1 + x)^2}$$

One teacher wanted to use whiteboards, but there was insufficient money in the school's budget to acquire these, so instead, she placed sheets of letter-sized white card stock inside page protectors to provide a low-cost alternative. She realised that this was actually far more flexible than the whiteboards, because she was able to preprint different images on the inserts for specific lessons. When she was teaching maths, the insert could be a sheet of graph paper. When she was teaching geography, it could be a map of Australia.

Exit Passes

When questions require longer responses, teachers can use the exit passes described in chapter 2. Examples of exit pass questions are:

- Why can't you have a probability greater than 1?
- What is the difference between mass and weight?
- Why are historians concerned with bias when analysing historical sources?

Exit pass questions work best when there is a natural break in the instruction; the teacher then has time to read through the students' responses and decide what to do next. In the example in chapter 2, the teacher discarded the exit passes, but if students have written their names on the back of the card, the teacher can use the exit passes as place settings for the next period with that class. The teacher can either create homogenous groups, so that she can work with the students who are having the greatest difficulty, or create heterogeneous groups in which there is at least one student who provided a good answer. Of course, since the work hasn't been assessed, the students with the good answers don't know who they are, which leads to more open discussion.

All these techniques create student engagement while providing the teacher with evidence about the extent of each student's learning so that the teacher is able to adjust the instruction to better meet the students' learning needs. Of course, the quality of the evidence—and, therefore, the quality of the instructional adjustments—depends on the quality of the questions asked, and so the next section of this chapter looks in more detail at what kinds of questions work best.

Discussion Questions and Diagnostic Questions

The following is a question that might be used in a middle years mathematics classroom.

Look at the following sequence:

$$3, 7, 11, 15, 19, \ldots$$

Which is the best rule to describe the sequence?

    A. $n + 4$

    B. $3 + n$

    C. $4n - 1$

    D. $4n + 3$

Many students will select A; they see that each number in the sequence is four more than the number preceding it, so the rule must be "keep adding 4". Others choose B, because although rule A tells you to keep adding 4, it does not tell you where to start, whereas B indicates that the sequence starts with 3, and numbers are added to 3 to generate the remaining numbers in the sequence. Interestingly, students who choose either A or B often justify their choices by saying that their teacher told them that n could be any number! The disadvantage with both A and B is that generating, say, the hundredth term requires first generating the previous ninety-nine. (These kinds of rules are sometimes called "term-to-term rules" since they allow one to generate the next term from the previous term.) Rules C and D are based on the observation that the numbers in the sequence can be viewed as one fewer or three greater than the four times table. (These kinds of rules are sometimes called "position-to-term rules" since they allow one to generate each term simply by knowing its position.) Rule C allows one to find the hundredth term by multiplying 100 by 4 and subtracting 1 to get 399. Rule D works in the same way, except that one has to remember that the hundredth term is generated by setting n to 99, since the first term corresponds to setting n to 0, rather than 1, and then adding 3.

This question can lead to a valuable discussion in the mathematics classroom, since it allows the teacher to challenge the idea that mathematics is a right-or-wrong subject. For example, rules A and B can be thought of as correct even though they do not use the standard mathematical notation, but they are less powerful than rules C and D. Rules C and D are equivalent, but one can make an argument that C is more elegant than D because to find the hundredth term, one sets n to 100 with rule C, but one has to remember to set it to 99 with rule D.

Just because someone chooses rule C, that does not mean that he understands why rule C is superior to rule A, for example. A student may have chosen C because it looks more "mathematical". The teacher learns little just by seeing which of these alternatives students choose. She has to hear the reasons for the choices. That is why this question is a valuable *discussion* question, but it is not a good *diagnostic* question. It can lead to fruitful discussion in the class, but there is no point in asking this question unless you are going to have the discussion. If you don't have twenty minutes for the class discussion, it's probably not worth asking the question.

Consider, as an alternative, the following question.

In which of these right triangles does a² + b² = c²?

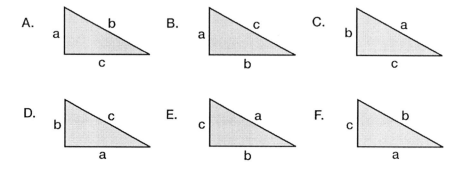

In some ways, this is a sneaky question, because there are two correct—and four incorrect—responses. In total, there are sixty-four possible choices of response to this question (for each of the six triangles, the student needs to decide whether the equation is true, so there are $2 \times 2 \times 2 \times 2 \times 2 \times 2$ possible combinations). Therefore, if students select B and D, and none of the others (provided they haven't copied these from other students), the teacher can be reasonably confident that they know how to apply Pythagoras' rule and can move on. Of course, if he has time, the teacher could decide to ask the students for the reasons for their choices, but the point is that, with this question, the teacher gains concrete evidence about the students' learning *without* having to have the classroom discussion.

The crucial feature of such *diagnostic* questions is based on a fundamental asymmetry in teaching; in general, it is better to assume that students do not know something when they do than it is to assume they do know something when they don't. What makes a question useful as a diagnostic question, therefore, is that it must be very unlikely that the student gets the correct answer for the wrong reason.

In science, a teacher might ask the following question to prompt discussion.

> Ice cubes are added to a glass of water. What happens to the level of the water as the ice cubes melt?
>
> A. The level of the water drops.
>
> B. The level of the water stays the same.
>
> C. The level of the water rises.
>
> D. More information is needed to be sure.

A teacher who has been focusing on Archimedes' principle hopes that the students choose B, but there are valid reasons for choosing alternatives. If evaporation is a significant factor, response A would be a better choice. The question does not specify that the ice cubes are floating. If so many cubes are added that they are resting on the bottom of the glass, then the water level will rise as the ice melts. Very able students may realise that B is not, in fact, correct—whatever the science teacher thinks. When ice melts, it draws heat from the surrounding water—it actually takes an appreciable amount of energy to convert ice at $0°C$ to water at $0°C$. So, as the ice melts, it cools the surrounding water by more than just the effect of the ice being colder than the water. If the water is above 4°C, then as it cools, it will contract, so A would then be correct (although the amount may be too small to measure). On the other hand, if the water is below 4°C, then cooling it will cause it to expand, so C would be correct. And since all these answers depend on the assumptions made, it is fair to claim that one needs more information to be sure, so D is correct, too. As with the previous question on sequences, the teacher learns little about the quality of his students' thinking just by seeing which response was chosen; the teacher needs to hear the reasons for the choices, so while this may be a good *discussion* question, it is a poor *diagnostic* question.

Consider the following question, developed by Mark Wilson and his colleagues at the University of California, Berkeley (Wilson & Draney, 2004, p. 149).

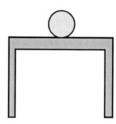

The ball sitting on the table is not moving. It is not moving because:

   A. No forces are pushing or pulling on the ball.
   B. Gravity pulls the ball down but the table is in the way.
   C. The table pushes up with the same force that gravity pulls down.
   D. Gravity is holding it on the table.
   E. There is a force inside the ball preventing it from rolling off the table.

The first response, A, is typically selected by students with the naïve conception that if there is no movement, then there are no forces in play. The second, B, on the other hand, looks quite reasonable. Is gravity pulling the ball down? Well, we might quibble about the language, but the ball is certainly being attracted by the gravitational pull of the earth, and the table is definitely in the way. So response B will be attractive to many students.

Response C is what the science teacher is hoping for. She has been teaching that when there is no movement, this could either mean that there are no forces acting on the object or, much more commonly, that the forces acting on the object are in equilibrium. Response D describes the situation in a similar way to response B, and response E is selected by students who, instead of seeing inertia as a property of matter, see it as a force (presumably at least in part because of the way the word *inertia* is used in everyday language).

The first and last responses, therefore, are obviously incorrect and related to well-known naïve conceptions that students have about the physical world. Response C is clearly the best answer, but what about B and D? They are correct, in an intuitive sense at least, so should the teacher accept either B or D as correct? In the science classroom, the answer is no. Responses B and D might be acceptable naïve ways of looking at the situation, but what the teacher is trying to establish is whether her students can think about this situation like a physicist. Physics is an unnatural way of thinking about the world—if it were natural, it wouldn't be so hard for students to learn. For example, when one ventures out in cold weather, it certainly feels as if the cold is coming in through one's clothes, but physicists have learned that it is more productive to think about the situation as one in which heat is escaping.

This question is not really asking, "What's happening here?" It is asking, "Can you think about this situation like a physicist?" And from that perspective, B and D are not acceptable. The only acceptable response is C. However, it is the plausibility of B and D that makes this such a valuable question. Students who are not secure in their understanding of forces will be tempted to opt for B or D, and so only students with a good understanding of the idea of forces in equilibrium will choose C. If a teacher asks this question, and students select C, then the teacher can be reasonably confident that they have understood the key idea about forces in equilibrium. She could, of course, ask students to explain the reasons for their choices and have a whole-class discussion, but this is not necessary for the teacher to gain valuable evidence about the students' understanding.

Discussion and diagnostic questions work in other school subjects, too. A history teacher might ask the following question.

In which year did World War II begin?

> A. 1937
>
> B. 1938
>
> C. 1939

D. 1940

E. 1941

Most Australian or European historians would probably select 1939, while Americans might regard the war as having started when they joined the conflict in 1941. However, interesting arguments can (and have!) also been made for 1937 (second Sino-Japanese war), 1938 (annexation of the Sudetenland), and 1940 (the Tripartite Pact). One particularly interesting feature of this question is that it focuses attention on the issue of what the phrase *world war* actually means. In 1939, Germany was at war with Britain and France, and Japan was involved in conflicts in Manchuria, but at that time, there was no formal alliance between Germany and Japan. However, even in 1939, the conflict was global in the sense that armed forces from British colonies such as India, Canada, Australia and New Zealand were involved, and German colonies in Africa bordered those of Britain and France.

Again, the point is that the teacher learns little about the quality of student thinking from hearing which answer a student chooses; the teacher needs to hear reasons for the choice, and that means hearing from every student in the classroom. That's great if you have time to hear from every student, but this kind of item is useless as a quick check on student understanding.

For a good example of a diagnostic question in history, consider the following question, which was mentioned as a possible exit pass question earlier.

Why are historians concerned with bias when analysing sources?

A. People can never be trusted to tell the truth.

B. People deliberately leave out important details.

C. People are only able to provide meaningful information if they experienced an event firsthand.

D. People interpret the same event in different ways, according to their experience.

E. People are unaware of the motivations for their actions.

F. People get confused about sequences of events.

This multiple-choice question was generated by using the most interesting incorrect responses from the exit passes. Most history teachers would agree that a class in which every student selects D as the best answer is probably ready to move on. Again, a discussion might be help-ful, but it is not necessary to help the teacher judge whether the students have understood the main point of this instructional sequence. It is the quality of the distractors that is crucial here—it is only because the distractors are so plausible that the teacher can reasonably conclude that the students who choose D have done so for the right reason.

The following item was generated by a group of English teachers from Cherry Hill, New Jersey, who were, at the time, teaching persuasive writing to their students.

Which of these is the best thesis statement?

    A. The typical TV show has nine violent incidents.

    B. The essay I am going to write is about violence on TV.

    C. There is a lot of violence on TV.

    D. The amount of violence on TV should be reduced.

    E. Some programs are more violent than others.

    F. Violence is included in programs to boost ratings.

    G. Violence on TV is interesting.

    H. I don't like the violence on TV.

Most English teachers would agree that D represents the best thesis statement *within the genre of persuasive writing*. If the writing were a factual reporting of a study on the amount of violence on TV, then response A might be a better thesis statement (analogous to an abstract for a research article) and F represents a perfectly reasonable opinion. Several of the other responses represent views that students hold, and, of course, the one that drives English teachers crazy is B—when students confuse a thesis statement with an introductory statement.

The following is an example from the teaching of modern foreign languages developed by a group of teachers of Spanish from Chico Unified School District, California.

Which of the following is the correct translation for "I give the book to him"?

    A. Yo lo doy el libro.

    B. Yo doy le el libro.

    C. Yo le doy el libro. Yo doy lo el libro.

    D. Yo doy el libro le.

E. Yo doy el libro lo.

Anyone who has taught Spanish to native English speakers knows that they have two particular difficulties in learning about pronouns: which pronoun to choose and where it should go. This item is ingenious because in one of the responses, the correct pronoun is in the wrong place; in another, the placement is correct, but the pronoun is incorrect; and in others, there are multiple errors. This question took quite a while to generate—certainly much more time than teachers would normally take to write a single question—but this question will still be a good question in twenty years' time, because native English speakers will still be having the same difficulty with pronoun selection and placement when learning Spanish.

Diagnostic questions can be used in a variety of ways. They can be used as "range-finding" questions to find out what students already know about a topic before beginning the instruction. A university teacher teaching an introductory course on botany poses the question "What proportion of the water taken in by the roots of a corn plant is lost through transpiration?" and asks the students to hold up one, two, three, four or five fingers according to whether they think the answer is 10 per cent, 30 per cent, 50 per cent, 70 per cent or 90 per cent. In teaching this course over many years, she has found that this simple question gives her a good indication of students' understanding of how plants work. Students who know little about plants assume that because plants die if they cannot get enough water in through the roots, the plants would seek to minimise the amount of transpiration in order to minimise water loss, and thus, they tend to select 10 per cent or 30 per cent. Students who understand the role played by water in transporting nutrients within the plant realise that most of the water taken in through the roots is lost through transpiration.

While using questions for range-finding at the beginning of a sequence of instruction is important, for many teachers, diagnostic questions are most useful in the middle of an instructional sequence to check whether students have understood something before moving on. The central idea here is that the teacher designs each lesson with at least one "hinge" in the instructional sequence. The hinge is a point at which the teacher checks whether the class is ready to move on through the use of a diagnostic question. How the lesson proceeds depends on the level

of understanding shown by the students, so the direction of the lesson hinges at this point.

While the design of diagnostic questions to be used at hinge points in lessons—*hinge-point questions* for short—is much more craft than science, work with teachers suggests that the following two principles are useful guidelines. First, it should take no longer than two minutes, and ideally less than one minute, for all students to respond to the question; the idea is that the hinge-point question is a quick check on understanding, rather than a new piece of work in itself. Second, it must be possible for the teacher to view and interpret the responses from the class in thirty seconds (and ideally half that time). If the teacher takes any longer than this to make sense of the students' responses, there is a risk of students getting off task and consequent disruptive behaviour.

The main requirement of good hinge-point questions is nicely illustrated by the following item, used as a sample item in the National Assessment of Educational Progress (NAEP, 2005) program for year four mathematics:

> **There are two flights per day from Newtown to Oldtown. The first flight leaves Newtown each day at 9.20 and arrives in Oldtown at 10.55. The second flight from Newtown leaves at 2.15. At what time does the second flight arrive in Oldtown?**

When I ask teachers how this item might be improved, they highlight the lack of information about whether these times are a.m. or p.m., the fact that the linguistic demands may be much more taxing than the mathematical demands for some students, the fact that one has to assume that both flights take exactly the same amount of time, and so on. These are all valid criticisms, but there is a much more fundamental problem with this item that, in my experience (and I have asked this of literally thousands of teachers), not one teacher in a hundred notices; students who think there are a hundred minutes in an hour and those who know there are just sixty get the same answer.

Earlier in this chapter, I proposed that there are two good reasons to ask questions in classrooms: to cause thinking and to provide the teacher with information that assists instructional decision making. Whether questions satisfy the first of these is relatively easy to evaluate. For the second, a key requirement of questions to assist instructional decision making is that students with the right idea about whatever it is we want them to know, understand, or be able to do should get different answers from students who do not have the right idea. Or, to put it another way, ideally it would be impossible for students to get the right answer for the wrong reason. One way to improve hinge-point questions is to involve groups of teachers. One group of teachers is given the task of developing a question, which is then handed to a second group of teachers whose task it is to try to identify a way in which a student might get the correct answer with incorrect reasoning. If they can, then the question is handed back to the first group to be refined.

In the case of the question about flights, one immediate improvement is simply to change the start time of the first flight from 9.20 to 9.05 (and presumably also to add a.m. or p.m.). With this modification, students who think there are one hundred minutes in an hour will get the answer 3.65, while those who know there are sixty minutes in an hour will answer 4.05. No question will ever be perfect, but by constantly seeking to understand the meaning behind students' responses to our questions, we can continue to refine and polish our questions and prompts.

A second requirement of questions to assist instructional decision making—much less important than the first but still useful to bear in mind when designing questions—is that the incorrect answers should be *interpretable*. That is, if students choose a particular incorrect response, the teacher knows (or at least has a pretty good guess) why they have done so. A multiple-choice question for which the incorrect responses relate to well-known naïve conceptions, such as the question on pronouns in Spanish, is one example.

While some people argue that multiple-choice questions have no place in educational assessment, there are good reasons for preferring the multiple-choice format for hinge-point questions. Multiple-choice questions are often criticised because they assess only low-order skills such as factual recall or application of a standard algorithm, although as the previous examples show, they can, if carefully designed, address higher-order skills. Another problem with multiple-choice questions used in tests is that there is no opportunity for the student to negotiate the meaning of the question with the question-setter or the machine that does the scoring.

In the classroom, these are much less important considerations, and multiple-choice questions have one great feature in their favour: the number of possible student responses is limited. When a teacher is faced with a sea of thirty whiteboards, each with a different response, it can be bewildering. Using multiple-choice questions provides a means for sorting all the students' responses ahead of time, so that precious classroom time is not spent trying to make sense of the students' answers.

Sometimes it makes sense to administer the question as a series of simple questions. For example, a primary school teacher has been teaching her students about lines of symmetry in two-dimensional shapes, and toward the end of the lesson, she displays the following images.

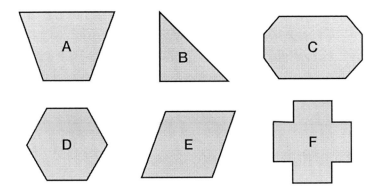

She calls out "A," and each student in the class has to hold up a number of fingers to show how many lines of symmetry shape A has. She then does the same for B, C, D, E and F. She doesn't try to remember how each student responds. Instead, she focuses on just two things:

1. Are there any items that a significant proportion of the class answers incorrectly and will need to be retaught with the whole class?

2. Which two or three students would benefit from individualised instruction?

Many students indicate that they think that shape D has just three lines of symmetry and that shape E has no lines of symmetry even though it is a rhombus. She points out to the class that D has six lines of symmetry, three through the corners and three through the midpoints of the sides, and reminds the class to look for lines of symmetry that are not horizontal, vertical or at 45°. She realises that the incorrect answers may not necessarily indicate poor mathematical understanding. After all, in the case of shape D, holding up just three fingers could be a result of students thinking that only one hand would be necessary, and as a result of the distortion of the data projector, the image of shape E might not actually be the rhombus shape intended. Nevertheless, she is well aware that in teaching, as noted previously, it is better to assume students do not know something when they do than to assume that they do know something when they don't.

In this episode, the teacher administered, marked and took remedial action regarding a whole-class quiz in a matter of minutes, without giving herself a pile of marking to do. She does not have a mark for each student to put in a markbook, but this is a small price to pay for such an agile piece of teaching. This is, in fact, a canonical example of formative assessment: the teacher engaged every student in the class by requiring them to indicate the number of lines of symmetry for each of the six shapes, and she used the information to make on-the-fly adjustments to her instruction.

There is one further benefit of focusing on high-quality questions, and that is their portability. Most teachers find worksheets or lesson plans developed by other teachers to be of limited usefulness. However, high-quality questions seem to work across different schools, regions, states, cultures and even languages. Indeed, sharing high-quality questions may be the most significant thing we can do to improve the quality of student learning.

Conclusion

Years ago, David Ausubel (1968) argued that the most important factor influencing learning is what the learner already knows and that the job of the teacher is to ascertain this and to teach accordingly. Students' conceptions are not random aberrations but the results of sophisticated and creative attempts to make sense of their experiences. Within a typical classroom, there is clearly not enough time for the teacher to treat each student as an individual, but with careful planning and the thoughtful application of the techniques presented in this chapter, the teacher can make the classroom a much more engaging place for students and one in which the teacher is able to make rapid and effective instructional adjustments to meet the learning needs of all students.

Once the teacher knows where learners are in their learning, she is in a position to provide feedback to the learners about what to do next—and this is the subject of the next chapter.

CHAPTER 5

Providing Feedback That Moves Learning Forward

It seems obvious that feedback to students about their work should help them learn, but it turns out that providing effective feedback is far more difficult than it appears. Much of the feedback that students get has little or no effect on their learning, and some kinds of feedback are actually counterproductive. This chapter reviews the research on feedback; why some kinds of feedback are, at best, useless and, at worst, actually lower performance; and how teachers can give their students feedback that moves learning forward.

The Quality of Feedback

The power of feedback to improve classroom learning was vividly demonstrated in a study by Maria Elawar and Lyn Corno (1985). A group of eighteen year six teachers in three schools in Venezuela received seven hours of training on how to provide constructive written feedback on the mathematics homework produced by their students. The feedback included specific comments on errors, suggestions to the students about how to improve, and at least one positive remark. A second group of teachers received the same training as the first group but gave constructive feedback to half their classes and just scores to the other half. A third group of teachers received no training and marked homework as normal (that is, by giving only scores). The students receiving the constructive feedback learned twice as fast as the control-group students—in other words, they learned in one week what the other students took two weeks to learn. Furthermore, in the classes given constructive feedback, the improvement in learning occurred across the achievement range, attitudes toward mathematics were more positive, and the achievement gap between male and female students was reduced (Elawar & Corno, 1985).

Ruth Butler (1988) investigated the effectiveness of different kinds of feedback on 132 year six students in twelve classes in four schools in Israel. For the first lesson, the students in each class were given a booklet containing a range of divergent thinking tasks in which students were asked to identify unusual uses for familiar objects (Torrance, 1962). At the end of the period, their work was collected. This work was then marked by researchers and teachers working independently. At the beginning of the next period, two days later, the students were given feedback on the work they had done in the first period. In the first classroom of each of the four schools, students were given scores: the lowest-quality work was given a score of 40; the highest-quality work was given a score of 99; and other work was given a score between these two extremes. In the second classroom in each of the four schools, students were given comments, such as "You thought of quite a few interesting ideas; maybe you could think of more ideas." In the third classroom in each of the four schools, the students were given both scores and comments. Then the students were asked to attempt some similar tasks and told that they would get the same sort of feedback as they had received for the first lesson's work. Again, the work was collected and scored.

Those given only scores made no progress from the first lesson to the second—their work was no better. When asked whether they wanted to continue doing similar work, those who had received high scores indicated that they did, but those who had received low scores did not. The students given only comments scored, on average, 30 per cent higher on the work done in the second lesson than that done in the first (although, of course, they did not know this because they had not been given scores), and all these students indicated that they wanted to carry on doing similar work. The obvious question is, What happened to the students given both scores and comments?

When I ask teachers what they think happened in this study, many assume that the students given both scores and comments progressed at least as much as those given comments. After all, if the comments alone produced a 30 per cent improvement in scores, then giving both scores and comments should have been even more informative.

Other teachers suggest that there was some trade-off between the two kinds of feedback. For example, some teachers say that they expect an improvement in scores because of the effects of the comments, but there may have been some polarisation of attitudes as a result of the scores; in other words, students who got high scores were motivated and wanted to carry on, while low scorers were demotivated and wished to move on to something else. A second possible trade-off works the other way, with students making no progress due to the effect of the scores but with attitudes kept positive by the encouragement provided by the comments.

Most teachers, therefore, are surprised to learn that the effect of giving both scores and comments was the same as the effect of giving scores alone. Far from producing the best effects of both kinds of feedback, giving scores alongside the comments completely washed out the beneficial effects of the comments; students who got high scores didn't need to read the comments, and students who got low scores didn't want to. And yet giving both a score (or mark) and some kind of comment is probably the most prevalent form of feedback to students in Australia. This study (and others like it, to follow) shows that if teachers are providing careful diagnostic comments and then putting a score or a mark on the work, they are wasting their time. They might as well just give a score or a mark—the students won't learn anything as a result, but the teacher will save a great deal of time.

Some clues as to why feedback can have these effects are provided by another study by the same researcher (Butler, 1987). This time, 200 year five and six students in eight classes spent a period working on a variety of divergent thinking tasks. Again, the work was collected and the students were given one of four kinds of feedback on this work at the beginning of the second period (again two days later):

1. In two classes, the students were given comments.

2. In two classes, the students were given marks.

3. In two classes, the students were given written praise.

4. In two classes, the students were given no feedback at all.

The quality of the work done in the second period was compared to that done in the first. The quality of the work of the students who had been given comments had improved substantially compared to their work in the first period, but those given marks and praise had made no more progress than those given absolutely no feedback on their work.

At the end of the second period, the students were given a questionnaire. The questionnaire sought to establish what factors influenced the students' decisions about whether to expend effort in the classroom and what factors the students believed determined whether they were successful or not. Specifically, the questionnaire was designed to elicit whether the students attributed their expenditure of effort and their success to ego-related factors or to task-related factors, as shown in table 5.1.

Table 5.1: Ego- and Task-Related Attributions

Attribution of	Ego	Task
Expenditure of effort	To do better than others To avoid doing worse than others	Interest To improve performance
Success	Ability Performance of others	Interest Effort Experience of previous learning

Students who were given comments had high levels of task-involvement, but their levels of ego-involvement were the same as those given no feedback. However, while those given written praise and those given marks had comparable levels of task-involvement to the control group, their levels of ego-involvement were substantially higher. As noted, the provision of marks and written praise had no effect on achievement; their only effect was to increase the sense of ego-involvement. This, as anyone involved in guidance and counselling work in schools knows, is bad news. To change a student's behaviour, it is generally far more effective to focus on criticising the behaviour rather than the student (in effect, giving task-involving rather than ego-involving feedback).

These findings are also consistent with research carried out in the 1970s that showed clearly that praise was not necessarily a good thing—in fact, the best teachers appear to praise slightly less than average (Good & Grouws, 1975). It is the quality rather than the quantity of praise that is important, and in particular, teacher praise is far more effective if it is infrequent, credible, contingent, specific and genuine (Brophy, 1981). It is also essential that praise is related to factors within an individual's control, so praising a gifted student simply for being gifted is likely to lead to negative consequences in the long term (Dweck, 2006).

The timing of feedback is also crucial. If it is given too early, before students have had a chance to work on a problem, then they will learn less. In a review of forty research reports on the effects of feedback in "test-like" events—such as questions embedded in programmed learning materials, review tests at the end of a block of teaching, and so on—Robert Bangert-Drowns, Chen-Lin Kulik, James Kulik and MaryTeresa Morgan (1991) found that what mattered was the degree of "mindfulness" in the students that the feedback generated. When students could peek ahead and look at answers to questions before they had tried to answer them, they learned significantly less than when they had to attempt to answer the question before getting feedback.

A direct demonstration of this was provided in a study by Malcolm Simmons and Peter Cope (1993). Pairs of students aged between nine and eleven worked on angle and rotation problems. Some students worked on the problems on a computer, using the programming language Logo, and some worked on the problems using pencil and paper. The students working in Logo were able to use a "trial and improvement" strategy that enabled them to get a solution with little mental effort. For those using pencil and paper, working out the effect of a single rotation was much more time consuming, giving these students an incentive to think carefully, and this greater "mindfulness" led to more learning.

The key idea in all this—that what matters is the mindfulness with which students engage in the feedback—means that sometimes less is more. A study of sixty-four year three students required the students to engage in arithmetical reasoning tasks and varied the kind of support they received. Half of the students were given a scaffolded response when they got stuck—in other words, they were given only the minimum amount of support to get them unstuck and to make progress. The other half of the students were given a complete solution to the problem on which they were stuck and then given a new problem to work on. Students given the scaffolded response learned more and retained their learning longer than those given full solutions (Day & Cordón, 1993). In a sense, this is hardly surprising, since those given the complete solutions had the opportunity for learning taken away from them. As well as saving the teachers time, developing skills of intervening as little as possible—just enough to get the students going—promotes better learning.

A good example of this kind of feedback is provided by Jonathon Saphier (2005):

> Teacher: "What part don't you understand?"
>
> Student: "I just don't get it."
>
> Teacher: "Well, the first part is just like the last problem you did. Then we add one more variable. See if you can find out what it is, and I'll come back in a few minutes." (p. 92)

Most teachers have had the experience of giving a student a new task only for the student to ask for help immediately. When the teacher asks, "What can't you do?" a common reply is, "I can't do any of it." In such circumstances, the student's reaction may be caused by anxiety about the unfamiliar nature of the task, and it is often possible to support the student by saying something like, "Copy out that table, and I'll be back in five minutes to help you fill it in." This is usually all the support the student needs. Copying out the table forces the student to look in detail at how the table is laid out, and this busywork can provide time for the student to make sense of the task herself.

Another good example of scaffolded feedback is provided by Ian Smith (2008). An art teacher had sketched a face and, in collaboration with the class, determined seven criteria for a successful portrait, including the idea that the eyes should be halfway down the face and that the distance between the eyes should be roughly the same as the width of one eye, and so on. She was then able to give feedback to a student in the format shown in figure 5.1.

✓	✗	✗	?	✗	✓	✓
1	2	3	4	5	6	7

Figure 5.1: Feedback grid for a face-drawing task.

This communicated clearly to the student what needed attention, took up very little of the teacher's time, and still left plenty of work for the student to do.

An obvious question that arises from these studies is, Does it make a difference whether the feedback is given orally or in writing? One of the few studies to address this was that of eighty Canadian students in three groups learning to write the major scales in their music classes (Boulet, Simard & De Melo, 1990). One group was given written feedback, a list of weaknesses and a work plan; the second group was given oral feedback on the nature of their errors, plus a chance to work on improvement in class; and the third group was given no feedback. At the beginning of the study, there were no differences between the three groups in terms of their previous achievements in music, scores on a test of musical aptitude, and on a measure of their ability to learn. All groups fell short of the mastery level of 80 per cent set for this task, but the students in the second group, who had been given oral feedback, scored significantly higher than the students in the other two groups (which were not significantly different from each other). Because the treatment of group 2 differed in three ways from that of group 1, it is not possible to determine what made the difference. However, from their observations, the researchers indicated that whether the feedback was given orally or in writing was much less important than the fact that group 2 was given time, in class, to use the feedback to improve their work.

Some types of feedback actually lower performance. Avraham Kluger and Angelo DeNisi looked at every study they could find that had ever been done on the effects of feedback in schools, universities and workplaces over a ninety-year period (from 1905 to 1995). They defined a feedback intervention as "actions taken by (an) external agent(s) to provide information regarding some aspect(s) of one's task performance" (Kluger & DeNisi, 1996, p. 255) and found over 3000 research studies (2500 journal articles and 500 technical reports) that looked at the impact of such feedback interventions on performance.

Of course, these studies varied in their quality, and to be sure that poor-quality studies were not being included, Kluger and DeNisi established a number of criteria for inclusion in their review. First, there had to be two groups of participants for whom the only difference (as far as could be judged) was whether they had received feedback or not. Second, a study had to have had at least ten participants (some, particularly in the medical field, had only a single participant). Third, the study had to include some kind of measurement of performance with sufficient details of the measurements of impact provided to be able to calculate the size of the impact of feedback on performance.

Astonishingly, only 131 of the original 3000 studies—approximately 4 per cent—satisfied these criteria of scientific quality. This figure was so low that Kluger and DeNisi reviewed the excluded studies to make sure that worthwhile studies were not being unduly rejected and concluded that those studies rejected could not shed useful light on the effects of feedback.

Just as surprisingly, in 50 of the 131 accepted studies, providing feedback actually lowered performance. In other words, in almost two out of every five carefully conducted studies, the participants would have done better if the feedback had not been given! To try to understand why feedback could have such counterproductive—and unexpected—effects, Kluger and DeNisi looked in detail at the studies to determine when feedback does and does not improve performance. They pointed out that when the feedback draws attention to a gap between one's current performance and the goal, what happens depends on whether the current performance is higher or lower than the goal.

When the feedback tells an individual that he has already surpassed the goal, one of four things can happen. Obviously one hopes that the individual would seek to change the goal to one that is more demanding, but it might also be taken as a signal to ease off and exert less effort. Also, when success comes too easily, the individual may decide that the goal itself is worthless and abandon it entirely or reject the feedback as being irrelevant.

When, as is more common, the feedback indicates that current performance falls short of the goal, there are again four responses. The recipient may change the goal, for example, when a student decides to settle for a B even though an A might be within her grasp but is felt to be too much work or too risky in terms of one's self-image to attempt. A second response is to abandon the goal altogether, as seen in the "learned helplessness" (Dweck, 1975) displayed by students who, in the face of repeated indications that they are falling short, decide that something is forever beyond them—for example, when a student says, "I'm no good at maths." The third type of response is to reject the feedback. This is quite common in workplace settings when, for example, someone who feels he has contributed well beyond what was expected gets a neutral evaluation from a supervisor. The effect of such rejection of feedback is to lower commitment (and therefore, possibly, to reduce performance). The fourth kind of response—and presumably the one intended by the person giving feedback—is to change one's behaviour so as to increase performance to match the goal. These responses to feedback are summarised in table 5.2.

Table 5.2: Possible Responses to Feedback

Response type	Feedback indicates performance exceeds goal	Feedback indicates performance falls short of goal
Change behaviour	Exert less effort	*Increase effort*
Change goal	*Increase aspiration*	Reduce aspiration
Abandon goal	Decide goal is too easy	Decide goal is too hard
Reject feedback	Ignore feedback	Ignore feedback

Only the two italicised responses are likely to improve performance. The other six, at best, do nothing and, at worst, lower performance, sometimes a considerable degree.

The research reviewed by Kluger and DeNisi (1996) also shows that it is very difficult, if not impossible, to predict which of these responses will occur. It will depend on the individual receiving the feedback, the kind of task on which feedback is given, and the recipient's perceptions of the person giving the feedback.

In concluding their review of the effects of feedback, Kluger and DeNisi point out that the biggest problem is the failure of most of the studies they reviewed to consider long-term effects. Even when the effect of feedback is to increase motivation, this may be a short-term improvement at the expense of a long-term worsening of performance. They suggest that, instead, research on feedback should focus less on the actual impact on performance and more on the kinds of responses that are triggered in the individual as a result of the feedback.

In a series of research studies spanning over thirty years, Carol Dweck of Stanford University and her colleagues have investigated, among other things, how students make sense of their successes and failures in school by asking students questions such as, "When you get an A, why is that?" or "If you got an F, why might that be?" Dweck and her colleagues found that there were three strong themes running through the students' responses (Dweck, 2000).

The first was whether the success or failure was due to factors relating to the individual or due to outside factors (in other words, how the attribution was *personalised*). For example, "I got an A because I did a good piece of work" would be an *internal* attribution because the cause is seen as being within the individual. "I got an F because Mr Smith hates me" would be an *external* attribution, because the cause is seen as being outside the individual. It is quite common to find individuals attributing their successes internally and their failures externally. There is an old Chinese adage that captures this tendency beautifully: "Success has a thousand fathers, but failure is an orphan."

The second theme was whether success was seen as being due to factors that were likely to be long lasting or transient (in other words, the permanence or stability of the factor). For example, when attributing success, "being smart" is likely to be seen by students as *stable* (that is, long lasting); if the student got an A this time because she is smart, she is likely to get an A next time because she will still be smart. If, on the other hand, a student says, "I got an A because I worked really hard on this assignment," then this is attributing success to an *unstable* (that is, transient) factor. Next time, whether the student gets an A will depend on how much effort he puts into the assignment.

The third was the *specificity* of the attribution: whether success or failure is seen as being due to factors that affect performance in all areas or just the area in question. For example, some students overgeneralise their successes. They believe that because they are told they are good at one thing, they are good at everything. Students can also overgeneralise failures and believe that because they fail at one thing, they are a failure at everything. (These are both *global* attributions.) Table 5.3 gives some examples of attributions of success and failure (see also Dweck, 2006).

Dweck (2000) and others have found that there is a slight tendency for boys to be more likely to attribute their successes to stable causes (such as ability) and their failures to unstable causes (such as lack of effort and bad luck). This would certainly explain the high degree of confidence with which many boys approach examinations for which they are rather unprepared. More controversially, the same research suggests that there is a slight tendency for girls to attribute their successes to unstable causes (such as effort) and their failures to stable causes (such as lack of ability), leading to the learned helplessness mentioned previously.

It is important to remember that these are not sharp differences between boys and girls—the overlap in how males and females attribute successes is far, far greater than the differences between males and

Table 5.3: Dimensions of Attributions of Success and Failure

Attribution	Success	Failure
Personalisation	Internal: "I got a good mark because it was a good piece of work." External: "I got a good mark because the teacher likes me."	Internal: "I got a low mark because it wasn't a very good piece of work." External: "I got a low mark because the teacher doesn't like me."
Stability	Stable: "I got a good mark because I'm good at that subject." Unstable: "I got a good mark because I was lucky in the questions that came up."	Stable: "I got a bad mark because I'm no good at that subject." Unstable: "I got a bad mark because I hadn't reviewed the material before the test."
Specificity	Specific: "I'm good at that, but that's the only thing I'm good at." Global: "I'm good at that, so I'll be good at everything."	Specific: "I'm no good at that, but I'm good at everything else." Global: "I'm useless at everything."

females—but these differences may in part explain why female students are now outperforming male students all over the world. The best learners consistently attribute both success and failure to internal, unstable causes. They believe: "It's up to me" (internal) and "I can do something about it" (unstable). The tendency is for girls to do this for their successes, although not for their failures, while the tendency for boys is to attribute neither successes nor failures to internal, unstable causes (successes tend to be attributed to internal stable causes, while failures tend to be attributed to external unstable causes). Regardless of the current tendencies, learning in classrooms will be considerably enhanced if students embrace this idea of "It's up to me, and I can do something about it." When I talk to students about these issues, I often use examples from sports, such as Michael Jordan, Tom Brady and Mike Piazza.

Although it is not true that Michael Jordan was cut from his secondary school varsity basketball team, he did experience a significant reversal. His secondary school, Lacey High School, ran a junior varsity team in addition to the main varsity team. Although the expectation was that most year ten students would play on the junior varsity team, some exceptionally gifted athletes in year ten did play on the varsity team. Jordan and his friend Leroy Smith attended a basketball camp in the summer after year nine and were encouraged by the coach of the varsity team, Pop Herring, to try for the varsity team in year ten. In the end, Smith made it, and Jordan did not. The assistant head coach at the time, Fred Lynch, said, "Leroy was not a better basketball player than Mike, he just had size. We didn't have a lot of tall kids, and Leroy was 6–6, 6–7 … and Pop Herring thought we had plenty of guards but needed size" (Pickeral, 2009). Although technically Jordan was not "cut" from the varsity team, the effect on him was galvanising, as he recalled in his acceptance speech when he was inducted into the National Basketball Association's hall of fame on 11 September, 2009: "Leroy Smith was the guy that when I got cut, he made the team […] he started the whole process with me, because when he made the team and I didn't, I wanted to prove—not just to Leroy Smith, not just to myself—but to the coach who actually picked Leroy over me—I wanted to make sure you understood, 'You made a mistake, dude'" (Jordan, 2009). In his junior and senior years, he did play for his secondary school's varsity team, and played well, amassing over 1400 points but not well enough to stand out nationally—at the end of his junior year, he was not on the list of the top 300 secondary school prospects being looked at by colleges (Bondy, 1999).

When Tom Brady was drafted into the National Football League in 2000, he wasn't drafted until the sixth round (he was actually the 199th player selected) and was the 7th quarterback chosen that year.

Perhaps most remarkably, when Mike Piazza was drafted by the LA Dodgers in 1988, he was drafted 1390th. In other words, the twenty-six Major League Baseball teams in existence at that time selected 1389 players ahead of him (and only 43 players after him!). He was the 63rd player drafted by the Dodgers that year, and he wasn't even drafted as a catcher (at the time, he was a first baseman). Realising that he probably had a better chance of a major league career as a catcher, he began playing catcher in the Winter Leagues, and played twenty-one games for the Anaheim Angels in 1992 (in which he batted a modest .232). In the following year, however, he was the National League's Rookie of the Year. Over the next fourteen years, he averaged over .300 and is now widely regarded as the best offensive catcher of all time, with career totals of 427 home runs and 1335 runs batted in.

Each of these three individuals received feedback that they weren't good enough, but each decided in the face of that feedback to improve rather than give up and do something else. The determination to do better was crucial in each of these cases.

Of course, whether a student sees feedback as relating to something that is permanent or transient depends on the student's attitude. One student may see feedback as sending the message "You're not smart enough," while another student may see the same feedback as saying, "You're not smart enough—yet." What matters is whether students see their future potential as limited by the current performance or not. Students who believe that ability is fixed will see any piece of work as a chance either to reaffirm their ability or to be shown up. If they are confident in their ability to achieve what is asked of them, then they will attempt the task. However, if their confidence in their ability to carry out their task is low, then they may well avoid the challenge (especially if they think others will succeed), and this can be seen in classrooms every day. A large number of students decide that, taking all things into account, they would rather be thought lazy than dumb and refuse to engage with the task. This is a direct consequence of the belief that ability is fixed. In contrast, those who see ability as incremental see all challenges as chances to learn—to get smarter—and, therefore, will try harder in the face of failure. These views of ability are generally not global—the same students often believe that ability in schoolwork is fixed and that ability in athletics is incremental, in that the more one trains at, say, triple jump, the more one's ability at that athletic endeavour increases. Therefore, what we need to do is ensure that the feedback we give students supports a view of ability as incremental rather than fixed: by working, you're getting smarter.

A Recipe for Future Action

All this suggests that providing effective feedback is very difficult. Get it wrong, and students give up, reject the feedback or choose an easier goal. Even when the students engage with the feedback, there is still a danger that the focus is shifted to short-term rather than long-term goals. That is why I have become more and more interested in the practices of high-achieving sports coaches.

In many secondary schools, those involved in academic programs treat the school as a talent refinery. Their job is to deliver the curriculum to the students. Some students will get it and thrive, and others will not. Although most states require a certain mark to be passed to qualify for a secondary school diploma (HSC, VCE, QCE, etc.), beyond that, if students cannot do well in a subject, then that's OK—it's obviously not their subject. In other words, the school functions rather like an oil refin-ery—its job is to sort the students into different layers. Those involved in athletics programs cannot afford to do this. The football coach does not have the luxury of saying, "We don't have a good enough full forward, so we're not going to play football this year." Instead, the football coach sees his job as making the best full forward they have as good as he can be, and doing the same at every other position. In other words, athletics coaches tend to see schools not as talent refineries but as talent incubators or talent factories. They see their job not as just identifying talent, but also nurtur-ing it, and even producing it, often getting out of athletes more than the athletes themselves believed they could achieve.

Coaches do this through the provision of *feedback that moves learn-ing forward*. In 1998, when Paul Black and I published "Inside the Black Box", we recommended that feedback during learning be in the form of comments rather than marks, and many teachers took this to heart. Unfortunately, in many cases, the feedback was not particu-larly helpful. Typically, the feedback would focus on what was defi-cient about the work submitted, which the students were not able to resubmit, rather than on what to do to improve their future learning. In such situations, feedback is rather like the scene in the rearview mirror rather than through the windshield. Or as Douglas Reeves once memo-rably observed, it's like the difference between having a medical and a postmortem.

Feedback functions formatively *only if the information fed back to the learner is used by the learner in improving performance*. If the information fed back to the learner is intended to be helpful but cannot be used by the learner in improving her performance, it is not formative. I remem-ber talking to a middle years student who was looking at the feedback his teacher had given him on a science assignment. The teacher had written, "You need to be more systematic in planning your scientific inquiries." I asked the student what that meant to him, and he said, "I don't know. If I knew how to be more systematic, I would have been more systematic the first time." This kind of feedback is *accurate*—it is describing what needs to happen—but it is not *helpful* because the learner does not know how to use the feedback to improve. It is rather like telling an unsuccessful comedian to be funnier—accurate, but not particularly helpful, advice.

Again, the differences in such practices between academic and athletic programs are illuminating. Imagine a young fast-pitch softballer is struggling—her earned run average (ERA) is 10 (if you know nothing about fast-pitch softball, that's not very good). If her coach were like many secondary school teachers, he might say, "Here's my advice: you need to get your ERA down." Accurate but not helpful. She knows she needs to get her ERA down, but she needs to know *how*.

The coach might look at her pitching and realise that the reason she is having a lot of runs hit off her is because she is trying, unsuccessfully, to pitch a rising fastball. This is a fastball thrown with so much rotation on the ball that as it reaches the plate, it rises sharply and is quite unhittable. Of course, if it doesn't rise, it's just a fastball over the middle of the plate, which is why she is getting hit for a lot of runs. So the coach says to the pitcher, "I know what's going wrong. It's your rising fastball. It's not rising." Again, accurate but not helpful.

But if the coach tells the pitcher that she is not dropping her pitching shoulder enough to deliver the pitch from below the knee, then this gives the athlete something to work with. The secret of effective feedback is that saying what's wrong isn't enough; to be effective, feedback must provide a *recipe for future action*.

This is actually inherent in the origin of the term *feedback*—a term borrowed from engineering. The term was first used by Norbert Wiener in 1946, and the important feature of feedback as it is used in engineering is that it forms part of a feedback *loop*. The classic example of a feedback loop is the regulation of the temperature in a room with the use of a thermostat.

The system has four key elements:

1. A means of setting the desired state (temperature setting)

2. A means of establishing the current state (thermometer)

3. A means of comparing the current state with the desired state (thermostat)

4. A means of bringing the current state in line with the desired state (furnace or cooling system)

For engineers, feedback about the discrepancy between the current state and the desired state is useless unless there is also a mechanism within the feedback loop to bring the current state closer to the desired state. In education, we use the term *feedback* for any information given to students about their current achievements. Just telling the students that their current performance falls short of where they need to be isn't feedback that an engineer would recognise. If there is nothing connecting the thermostat to the furnace, then there is no feedback loop and, therefore, to an engineer, no feedback.

To be effective as a recipe for future action, the future action must be designed so as to progress learning. In other words, the feedback must embody a model of progression, and here, again, is where much coaching in athletics programs is well designed. It is not enough to clarify the current state and the goal state. The coach has to design a series of activities that will move athletes from their current state to the goal state. Often coaches will take a complex activity, such as the double play in baseball, and break it down into a series of components, each of which needs to be practised until fluency is reached, and then the components are assembled together. Not only does the coach have a clear notion of quality (the well-executed double play), he also understands the *anatomy* of quality; he is able to see the high-quality performance as being composed of a series of elements that can be broken down into a developmental sequence for the athlete. This skill of being able to break down a long learning journey—from where the student is right now to where she needs to be—into a series of small steps takes years for even the most capable coaches to develop. The best coaches say they are always learning how to be better at coaching. There are clear principles that can guide their development, which are discussed later in the chapter, together with some practical techniques for classroom implementation.

Marking

From the research discussed previously, it should be clear that the marking practices prevalent in most middle years schools and secondary schools are actually lowering student achievement. Worse, typical marking practices don't even do the one thing they are supposed to do, which is tell us what students know:

> Imagine, for a moment, a school that has an eight-week marking period, with students receiving a mark each week. Lesley starts out with four *A*s but ends up with four *C*s. Overall, of

course, she gets a *B*. Chris, on the other hand, starts out with four *C*s but ends up with four *A*s. He gets a *B* too.

But who has learned more? In terms of overall achievement, Chris, with his four final *A*s, seems to have mastered the content for the marking period and really deserves an *A*. Conversely, Lesley, with her four final *C*s, seems far from mastering the content, but she gets a *B* because of her good start. The fact is that our current marking practises don't do the one thing they are meant to do, which is to provide an accurate indication of student achievement. (Clymer & Wiliam, 2006/2007, p. 36)

We can't get rid of marks—the whole system of university selection relies on them—but what we can do is design smarter marking systems that provide accurate information about student achievement while supporting student learning. The key to doing this is a principle outlined by Alfie Kohn (1994): "Never mark students while they are still learning" (p. 41). As soon as students get a mark, the learning stops. We may not like it, but the research reviewed here shows that this is a relatively stable feature of how human minds work. So we have to deal with it and design assessment systems accordingly.

If mark stop learning, students should be given them as infrequently as possible. In secondary school, there may be an argument for one per marking period but certainly no more. In the middle years, there may be a case for marks once a year, but in primary school, the use of marks appears to be entirely unjustified.

Many administrators realise this but continue to mandate marks because they believe that parents want them, and surveys of parents often show support for marks, but this is hardly an informed choice. Parents often support marks only because they want to know how their children are doing in school and assume that marks are the only way to find out. However, parents have no idea what their children's marks mean, because, as Paul Dressel remarked over half a century ago, "A mark can be regarded only as an inadequate report of an inaccurate judgment by a biased and variable judge of the extent to which a student has attained an undefined level of mastery of an unknown proportion of an indefinite material" (Dressel, 1957, p. 6). Once we have them hooked, students want marks, too, but rather than allowing them to become codependents in an unhealthy relationship, it would surely be better not to get students addicted to marks in the first place.

We need classroom assessment systems that are designed primarily to support learning and deal in data that are recorded at a level that is useful for teachers, students and parents in determining where students are in their learning. Such fine-scale evidence can always be aggregated for summative reporting. It is not possible to go the other way: from aggregate reports of achievement to learning needs.

For example, a swimming teacher was observing students in a swimming pool. She had drawn a grid listing the students' names in the first column. The other four columns were headed: arms, legs, breathing and timing. As she observed each student, she entered a 0, 1 or 2 in each column, according to the level of competence displayed by the student in that aspect of swimming. She could, if she wanted to, add up the scores and give each student a total out of eight, but knowing that someone has scored seven out of eight is useless for planning instruction. On the other hand, knowing that a student's arms, legs and breathing are fine but the timing requires attention is useful to the teacher (and would also be useful to another teacher if one had to take over teaching this group).

Middle years science specialist Jacki Clymer and I described how these principles could be implemented in a science classroom (Clymer & Wiliam, 2006/2007). For each marking period, the key learning outcomes are identified. For example, for the first marking period, a total of ten areas of interest are adopted (some of these might cover multiple learning outcomes):

1. The appropriate use of laboratory equipment

2. Metric unit conversion and labelling

3. Calculating density

4. Applying density (floating, sinking, layering, thermal expansion)

5. Density as a characteristic property

6. The phases of matter (at a molecular level)

7. Gas laws

8. Communication (graphing)

9. Communication (lab reports)

10. Inquiry skills

For each of the ten areas of interest, sources of evidence are identified. For example, the evidence for the appropriate use of laboratory equipment comes from observations, from a homework assignment on safety, and from the laboratory reports completed by the students. On the basis of the evidence collected, the teacher scores each area for each student as either 0 (no evidence of mastery), 1 (some evidence of mastery) or 2 (strong evidence of mastery), and keeps these data in a spreadsheet. The teacher uses the "conditional formatting" feature in the spreadsheet to highlight a cell in green if there is a 2 in the cell, yellow if there is a 1, and red if there is a 0. The result is an instant summary of the achievement of the class, as shown in figure 5.2 (page 126).

Since there are ten areas for this marking period, each student's total is divided by twenty to yield a percentage, which can then be used to provide an indication of what the mark would be if the marking period ended at that point. However, at any time before the end of the marking period, students can provide further evidence of their competence. So, for example, if Emma Bettany wants to know what she needs to do to get an A, the teacher can quickly tell her that all she needs to do is provide evidence that she has mastered one of the three areas for which the teacher has, to date, seen only evidence of partial mastery.

At the end of the marking period, the students take a test, which is used to confirm the evidence collected up to that point. When the performance on the test indicates a different level of mastery from that indicated on the basis of the class work, this is treated as a matter needing further investigation (rather than, for example, just averaging the scores). Typically, the teacher will interview the student to probe the extent of the student's understanding of the matter in question.

Perhaps the most profound impact of such a marking system is that it pushes both teacher and students into thinking about longer-term learning. If a student shows mastery of something at the beginning of the marking period but then fails to do so later, his mark can go down.

This is exactly what we found in a study of the implementation of this system with a year eight class. Students became more engaged in monitoring their own learning; frequently asked for clarification, both from the teacher and from their peers; and regarded the teacher more as a coach than a judge. Their achievement went up, too (Clymer & Wiliam, 2006/2007).

Last name	First name	Use equipment	Metric units	Calc. density	Apply density	Density property	Phases of matter	Gas laws	Comm. (graphs)	Comm. (reports)	Inquiry skills	%	Mark
Period		1	1	1	1	1	1	1	1	1	1		
	Outcome	1	2	3	4	5	6	7	8	9	10		
Allen	James	2	2	2	1	2	2	2	1	1	0	75%	C
Ayears	Liam	2	2	2	2	2	1	1	1	0	1	65%	D
Baldwin	Lee	1	2	2	2	2	2	2	1	1	0	75%	C
Bettany	Emma	2	2	1	2	2	2	2	2	1	1	85%	B
Birch	Leah	2	1	2	2	2	2	1	1	0	0	65%	D
Burns	Robert	2	2	1	1	2	0	1	1	0	0	50%	D
Cobern	David	2	2	2	2	2	2	2	1	0	1	80%	B
Creasey	Simon	1	1	2	2	2	2	1	1	0	0	65%	D
Darby	Hannah	1	2	2	2	2	2	1	2	1	1	80%	B
Eastwood	Luke	1	2	1	2	2	1	2	1	0	0	60%	D
Ferguson	Mark	2	2	2	2	2	2	2	2	0	1	85%	B
Forbes	Sarah	1	0	1	0	2	1	2	1	0	0	40%	D
Goodger	Mark	2	2	2	2	2	2	2	2	2	1	95%	A
Hall	Mark	1	2	2	2	1	2	2	2	2	1	85%	B
Howells	Georgie	2	2	2	2	2	1	2	1	0	0	70%	C
Hudson	Kirsty	2	2	1	2	2	1	2	1	0	0	65%	D
Hurley	Victoria	1	2	0	0	2	1	2	0	0	2	50%	D
Langan	Jennifer	2	2	2	2	2	2	2	2	1	1	90%	A
Larkin	Andrew	1	1	0	2	2	1	2	2	0	0	55%	D
Leach	Jonathan	2	2	1	2	2	2	1	2	0	1	75%	C
Lowings	Charlottte	1	1	0	2	2	2	2	1	2	1	75%	C
Mcglashan	Scott	1	2	1	1	2	1	2	0	0	0	50%	D
Parr	Amy	2	1	1	2	2	1	2	2	1	0	75%	C
Ringham	Grace	0	1	0	2	2	1	1	1	0	0	40%	D
Rosamond	Lee	1	2	2	2	2	2	2	1	0	0	70%	C
Rose	Peter	1	2	1	2	2	1	2	2	1	1	80%	B
Ryder	Thomas	2	1	2	1	2	1	2	2	0	1	70%	C
Skeats	William	1	2	2	1	2	2	2	2	2	2	90%	A
Walton	Emma	2	2	2	2	2	2	2	2	2	2	100%	A
Average facility		76%	86%	71%	84%	98%	78%	88%	69%	29%	31%		

Figure 5.2: Marking scheme based on Clymer and William, 2006/2007.

A particularly important feature of this marking system is that it avoids the ratchet effect present in most marking systems—the idea that a student's mark for a particular piece of work can never go down. When students are allowed multiple resubmissions and can improve work without penalty, this can have negative consequences. For example, in many secondary schools, students know they can hand in very poor quality work, get feedback on it and improve it for a passing mark. The problem with such systems is that there is no incentive for students to make the first submission as good as it can be, because it can always be remediated in a second submission. Schools that allow students to resubmit work multiple times need to consider creating systems that avoid such problems. Deanna Holen, a physical education teacher in Chico, California, designed a marking rubric that was constructed in such a way that no matter how poor the original submission, a resubmission could bring it up to a passing mark, but it also ensured that the better the first submission was, the higher the final mark would be, as shown in table 5.4 (page 128).

Another way to provide similar incentives is to allocate 50 per cent of the available points to the first submission and 50 per cent to the improvement shown in the work as a result of responding to the feedback.

Some teachers question whether we should ever be satisfied with any work that is not of a high standard. Joe Rubin, a science teacher in San Francisco, only gives one mark: an A. When he marks work, it either comes back with an A or is returned with a note saying it is not yet ready to be evaluated. Of course, the students who need multiple attempts to get an A may well run out of time, and thus complete fewer assignments, but the message this teacher is sending to all students is that only the best is good enough. More importantly, he sends the message that everyone can do quality work, although some need more support and guidance than others. He emphasises quality over quantity.

Practical Techniques

If I had to reduce all of the research on feedback into one simple overarching idea, at least for academic subjects in school, it would be this: feedback should cause thinking. All the practical techniques discussed here work because, in one way or another, they get the students to think, rather than react emotionally to the feedback they are given. When I talk to teachers about the first of the two studies by Ruth Butler

Table 5.4: Marking Scheme to Encourage Both Improvement and Good First Attempts

Mark on first submission

		A	B	C	D	F
Mark on second submission	A	A	A	B	C	C
	B	B	B	C	C	D
	C	C	C	C	D	D
	D	D	D	D	D	F
	F	F	F	F	F	F

and her colleagues discussed previously (the one in which students were given comments, scores or both), I ask them, "When the students were given both comments and scores, which did they look at first?" Everyone realises, of course, that it was the score. What is more interesting is what the students looked at next: somebody else's score.

As soon as students compare themselves with someone else, their mental energy becomes focused on protecting their own sense of well-being rather than learning anything new. In one school I have worked with, the principal insists that there is a score or a mark on each student's work every two weeks. The English teachers give students the traditional letter marks at the end of each marking period, but during the marking period, they use a marking scheme that they call "minus, equals, plus". As well as comments, each student receives a symbol of –, = or + depending on whether the work submitted was not as good as, about the same as, or better than his or her last work on the topic. The students who used to get A marks hate it, because they have to keep getting better to get a +. It is particularly interesting when high-achieving students in these classes compare their marks with other students' and find that they have received = or even – when students with lower absolute achievement get a +. The important feature of such a marking scheme is that it feeds back to learners about things that are within their control, such as whether they are improving, rather than things that are not within their control, such as how they compare with other students in the class.

To be effective, feedback needs to direct attention to what's next rather than focusing on how well or badly the student did on the work, and this rarely happens in the typical classroom. Pam Hayes, a middle years maths teacher, told me about a conversation she had with a year five student in which the student said, "When you get a lot of feedback on your work, it means it wasn't very good." When asked to explain this rather surprising comment, the girl pointed out that successful work is usually just given a (high) mark and a comment like "Good job," whereas less successful work is returned to the student with lots of annotation from the teacher. To this girl, the more "feedback" you got, the worse your work must have been. In many classrooms, teachers require students to do corrections for homework, leaving high achievers with nothing to do. Used in this way, feedback really is punishment.

If, however, we embrace the idea of feedback as a recipe for future action, then it is easy to see how to make feedback work constructively: don't provide students with feedback unless you allow time, in class, to work on using the feedback to improve their work. Then feedback is not an evaluation of how well or how badly one's work was done but a matter of "what's next?"

One technique for structuring this that is particularly effective when responding to a piece of student writing is called "three questions". As the teacher reads each student's work, when she sees something on which she would like the student to reflect, she places a numbered circle at that point in the text. Underneath the student's work, the teacher writes a question relating to the first numbered circle, leaves a number of lines for the student's response, writes a question for the second, leaves space for the student's response, and then writes a third question. The first ten or fifteen minutes of the next lesson are taken up with responding to the three questions posed by the teacher. The important feature of this technique is that no matter how bad or good your work was, everyone has the same amount of work to do.

This idea that feedback is about "what's next?" also addresses another shortcoming of much current practice. I often ask teachers whether they believe that their students spend as much time utilising the feedback they are given as it has taken the teacher to provide it. Typically, fewer than 1 per cent of teachers believe this to be the case, and this needs to change. The first fundamental principle of effective classroom feedback is that feedback should be more work for the recipient than the donor.

Giving students comments, rather than marks or scores, is obviously useful, but most teachers still find it difficult to get the students to read the comments. Charlotte Kerrigan, an English teacher, had been giving only comments to her students for a while but was still unhappy with the amount of attention the students were giving to her comments, so she made a small but extremely powerful change in the way she provided feedback. Her year ten class had just completed essays on a Shakespeare play they had been studying. Kerrigan collected the essays, and instead of writing her comments in the students' notebooks, she did so on strips of paper. Each group of four students received their four essays and the four strips of paper, and the group had to decide which comment belonged with which essay.

A second principle of effective feedback is that it should be focused. We generally give our students large amounts of what we call feedback (although an engineer probably wouldn't), but it is usually of moderate quality, and we generally don't require students to do much with it. In giving feedback, less is often more.

I learned this the hard way when I first became a teacher educator, working with preservice teachers and observing them during their periods of practical teaching. I would sit at the back of their classrooms and assiduously note all the errors they had made in their teaching—I would frequently generate as many as three pages of comments on all the errors the student-teacher had made in a forty-five-minute lesson. At the end of the period, I would bestow this wonderful feedback on the hapless student. I was frustrated that my wonderful feedback did not seem to be having any effect. After a while, I realised that the problem was that I was giving far too much feedback; I needed to give less, but more focused, feedback. Rather than handing over a whole list of errors to be corrected, I started saying things like, "Over the next two weeks, I want you to work on these two things: first, before you give any important instructions to the class, make them put their pens down, and second, make sure that you don't talk over the students—if they start talking to each other when you are talking, stop talking." I gave less feedback and had more impact by being more focused.

A third principle is that the feedback should relate to the learning goals that have been shared with the students. If the teacher has provided a scoring rubric, then it is important that the feedback relates to that rubric. If there are learning intentions and success criteria for the work, then the feedback should loop back to those. This sounds obvious, but I have lost count of the number of times I have seen teachers provide students with rubrics or success criteria and yet fail to use these in framing their feedback to the students.

Maths teachers may be thinking that ideas such as comment-only marking may work well in English and social studies, but maths is different. After all, if a student has solved twenty equations, and the teacher places a tick mark next to fifteen of them and a cross next to the other five, the student can work out his score of fifteen out of twenty, even if the teacher does not put a score of 75 per cent on the work. As noted previously, however, what is important is not the form that the feedback takes but the effect it has on students.

Putting a tick or a cross next to each of the solutions leaves nothing for the student to do, except maybe correct those that are incorrect. An alternative would be to say to the student, "Five of these are wrong. You find them; you fix them."

This technique is particularly well suited to mathematics as it is often easier to check whether a solution is correct (for example, by substituting for a solved variable back into the original equation). However, it can also be readily adapted to other subjects. When reviewing a final draft of a piece of writing, an English teacher placed a dot in the margin of each line where there was something that needed attention. For weaker students, she replaced the dot with a *g* for an error in grammar, an *s* for a spelling error, a *p* for punctuation and so on, thus differentiating the feedback. The important point is that the feedback is focused, is more work for the recipient than the donor, and causes thinking rather than an emotional reaction.

Conclusion

The word *feedback* was first used in engineering to describe a situation in which information about the current state of a system was used to change the future state of the system, but this has been forgotten, and any information about how students performed in the past is routinely regarded as useful. It is not. In this chapter, we have seen that in almost two out of every five carefully designed scientific studies, information given to people about their performance lowered their subsequent performance. We have also seen that when we give students feedback, there are eight things that can happen, and six of them are bad (table 5.2, page 115).

Some ways to give effective feedback have been described in this chapter, but every teacher will be able to come up with many more, provided that the key lessons from the research on feedback are heeded. If we are to harness the power of feedback to increase student learning, then we need to ensure that feedback causes a cognitive rather than an emotional reaction—in other words, feedback should cause thinking. It should be focused; it should relate to the learning goals that have been shared with the students; and it should be more work for the recipient than the donor. Indeed, the whole purpose of feedback should be to increase the extent to which students are owners of their own learning, which is the focus of the next two chapters.

CHAPTER 6

Activating Students as Instructional Resources for One Another

Even though there is a substantial body of research that demonstrates the extraordinary power of collaborative and cooperative learning, it is rarely deployed effectively in classrooms. This chapter explores the role that learners can play in improving the learning of their peers and concludes with a number of specific classroom techniques that can be used to put these principles into practice.

Cooperative Learning

Having reviewed the evidence, Robert Slavin, Eric Hurley and Anne Chamberlain (2003) concluded that "research on cooperative learning is one of the greatest success stories in the history of educational research" (p. 177). Exactly why cooperative learning has such a profound effect is still a matter of some debate, although there appear to be four main factors:

1. Motivation. Students help their peers learn because, in well-structured cooperative learning settings, it is in their own interests to do so, and so effort is increased.

2. Social cohesion. Students help their peers because they care about the group, again leading to increased effort.

3. Personalisation. Students learn more because their more able peers can engage with the particular difficulties a student is having.

4. Cognitive elaboration. Those who provide help in group settings are forced to think through the ideas more clearly.

All these factors have a role to play, but some appear to be more powerful than others. In particular, just focusing on social cohesion, without attending to the other factors, appears to have little impact on student learning. A review of ninety-nine studies found that cooperative learning in which group rewards depended on the *aggregate* of the learning of *individual* members produced four times the impact on learning than was found when rewards were based on a single group product (Slavin, 1995).

Personalisation and cognitive elaboration are important, too. A review of seventeen studies of peer interaction on the learning of mathematics in primary, middle years and secondary schools found that help in the form of answers or procedural information had no benefit for those giving help and produced a significant drop in the achievement of those getting help. On the other hand, when the help took the form of elaborated explanations, both those giving and getting help benefited, and this benefit was especially great for those giving help, producing at least a 50 per cent increase in the rate of learning (Webb, 1991).

One particularly surprising finding is that the effect of peer tutoring can be almost as strong as one-on-one instruction from a teacher. A study of 109 students in year four, five and six classrooms found that students working in student-led groups learned almost as much as students getting one-on-one tutorial instruction from a teacher, and those in student-led groups actually learned more than those in teacher-led groups (Schacter, 2000).

In fact, under certain circumstances, peer tutoring can actually be more effective than one-on-one tutorial instruction from a teacher. Some time ago, I asked two year five girls whether they preferred to get help from the teacher or from each other. One of the girls said, "I much prefer to get help from my friends because teachers have got this weird kind of language, if you know what I mean." This didn't surprise me as most teachers have had the experience of giving what they think is a perfectly lucid explanation of something to a student only for the student to respond with, "Huh?" More galling, often a peer will contribute something that seems completely unintelligible and the student says, "Oh right, I get it now." The fact that students have a kind of shorthand communication is nothing new. What was surprising was what the girl said next. She said, "And if I haven't understood it after the second explanation from the teacher, I pretend I have." I asked her why she did this, and she said it was because she was aware of how busy the teacher was and didn't want to take up too much of her time. Her friend admitted that she did this, too. I then interviewed some boys who also said that they pretended that they understood something when in fact they didn't, typically not out of concern for the teacher's time but because they did not want to appear foolish in front of the teacher.

As a result of these conversations, I started looking at the expressions on the faces of students when the teacher was engaged with them in one-on-one tutorial instruction, and I realised that they couldn't wait for the ordeal to end. Hardly ever would a student interrupt a teacher for clarification or to ask the teacher to go over something a second time. And yet, when working with peers, a student would ask the peer to slow down or to go over something again and again until it was understood. Peer tutoring can, under the right circumstances, generate more effective learning than would be possible with one adult for every student, because of the change in power relationships.

Effective cooperative learning requires the presence of two elements. First, there must be group goals, so that students are working as a group, not merely working in a group. Second, there must be individual accountability, so that individual students cannot be carried along by the work of others.

Some studies have found that the benefits of cooperative learning environments are greater for lower achievers (for example, Boaler, 2002); others have found benefits for high achievers (for example, Stevens & Slavin, 1995). Overall, it appears that, as long as the two key features of group goals and individual accountability are present, cooperative learning is equally effective for students at all achievement levels (Slavin, Hurley & Chamberlain, 2003). Having said that, cooperative learning interventions seem to be particularly beneficial for students of colour at the undergraduate level (Springer, Stanne & Donovan,

1999), and the value of collaborative learning environments for African American students in particular has been emphasised by Wade Boykin and his colleagues (Boykin, Coleman, Lilja & Tyler, 2004; Boykin, Lilja & Tyler, 2004).

Although the two requirements—group goals and individual accountability—seem straightforward, they cut across some widely held assumptions about fairness for groups and individuals. For example, most teachers accept as fair the idea of group rewards for behaviour. A technique that some schools use to promote good behaviour in classrooms is "secret student". The idea is that each day, one member of the homeroom is selected at random by the homeroom teacher as the secret student, but the identity of the secret student is revealed only to the teachers teaching that particular student that day. Each teacher then tells the homeroom teacher whether the behaviour of the secret student was satisfactory, and if the proportion of periods in which the behaviour of the secret student exceeds a prespecified threshold (for example, 80 per cent, all but one or all but two), then the class is credited with a good day and the identity of the secret student is revealed to the class. If, however, the behaviour of the secret student is not good enough, then the identity of the student is *not* revealed. The class receives some group reward that depends on the number of good days that are recorded.

While one might have some concerns about the operation of the secret-student scheme in practice, the use of peer pressure in this way seems to be broadly acceptable and certainly more acceptable than such a scheme would be if applied to academic work.

For example, a middle years science teacher has arranged her class into groups of four students, and each group is assigned the task of learning about continental drift by studying a chapter in a textbook. The students are provided with study guides and an indication of the success criteria for the task. At the end of the week, the class is given a quiz on this material, and each group is given the score achieved by the lowest-scoring member of the group (of course, the name of the lowest-scoring member is not revealed). In other words, the group is characterised by the achievement at the "trailing edge".

Many teachers find this type of assessment completely unacceptable. They point out that the score awarded to the group, being that of the lowest-scoring member, is unrepresentative of the level of the achievement of the group, which is an entirely fair point. It would certainly be invalid to infer anything about the achievement of individual members of the group from this score, and it would be quite wrong to enter this score in a markbook as an indication of the achievements of individual members of the group. But if, instead, the score is taken as an indication of how well the group worked *as a group*, then the awarded score seems more reasonable.

The fact that many teachers view secret student as entirely legitimate but trailing-edge scoring as unacceptable reveals how difficult it is to secure the benefits of cooperative learning in classrooms. In fact, what teachers describe as cooperative learning in their classrooms rarely has the features that would make it effective. One survey of eighty-five primary school teachers in two regions found that although 93 per cent of the teachers said they employed collaborative learning, follow-up interviews with twenty-one of the teachers showed that only five teachers implemented collaborative learning in such a way as to create both group goals and individual accountability (Antil, Jenkins, Wayne & Vadasy, 1998). Furthermore, only one of the twenty-one teachers implemented collaborative learning that satisfied the more complex criteria proposed by Elizabeth Cohen (1994), namely open-ended tasks that emphasise higher-order thinking, group tasks that require input from other members, multiple tasks related to a central intellectual theme, and roles assigned to different group members.

Practical Techniques

The remainder of this chapter presents a number of techniques that teachers have found useful in getting started with the process of activating students as learning resources for one another. Inevitably, a number of these techniques involve students assessing each other's work, and this raises a number of ethical concerns. Perhaps the most important is whether students should be involved in summative assessment, and in my view, the answer is a firm no. I think it is quite wrong for one student to be placed in the position of evaluating the achievement of another student for the purpose of reporting to parents or others. The purpose of peer assessment should be simply, and purely, to help the individual being assessed improve his work.

C3B4ME

In this technique, before a student is allowed to ask the teacher for help, assistance must have been sought from at least three other students, hence the description "see three before me". Some teachers support this with a poster declaring, "There is more than one teacher in this room."

Peer Evaluation of Homework

One middle years maths teacher has tried to reduce the amount of time she spends checking homework by involving the students more. When the students arrive, they don't know how the homework is going to be checked and marked. Sometimes the teacher gives the students a rubric, and they have to mark their own. Sometimes students are told to swap notebooks with a neighbour and mark each other's, and sometimes one group of four students is asked to look at the work of another group. When she began to implement this approach regularly, two surprising things happened. First, more students did the homework. If students had not completed the homework, then they were not allowed to participate in the group evaluation activity, and even though these students were, in effect, being allowed to do in class what they should have done at home, they regarded being excluded from the evaluation as sufficient punishment to ensure that next time they had something to be evaluated. Second, their work was neater. Students appeared to care more about communicating clearly with each other than about communicating to the teacher.

Homework Help Board

Another approach for dealing with issues arising from homework is the homework help board. At the beginning of the day (in primary school) or at the beginning of the lesson (in the middle years and secondary school), students indicate on the homework help board any questions that they had about the homework. Students who think they can help students who have questions about the homework are then encouraged to seek those students out and provide help.

Two Stars and a Wish

This is a very simple technique for getting started with peer assessment. When any student gives feedback on another student's work, he has to provide two things he thinks were good about the work (the two stars) and a suggestion for improvement (the wish). The comments are written on sticky notes so that if the recipient doesn't find the feedback helpful, it can easily be removed.

To improve the quality of the feedback, a teacher collected the sticky notes once the students had responded to the feedback and, using a document camera, displayed each note to the class (anonymously) and asked the class to vote on whether they thought that the comment would be useful to them. The class then discussed the salient features of the best-rated feedback, and the resulting criteria were displayed on a poster in the classroom for future reference.

End-of-Topic Questions

It is quite common for a teacher to reach the end of an exposition, a chapter or a unit and ask the class, "Any questions?" Of course, few students are willing to raise their hands to ask a question because they do not want to look foolish in front of the rest of the class. To overcome this, the teacher can say, "In your groups, decide if you have any questions." Just the chance to talk through the matter with their peers can make students more confident about asking questions in front of the class—after all, if no-one in the group has a solution, then it's clearly not a dumb question. Some teachers go even further and insist that each group comes up with at least one question. The teacher collects the questions, sorts them quickly, and deals with all the questions on the same issue at the same time. Gathering all the questions before beginning to answer the questions is particularly useful because it allows the teacher to make connections between different issues that the students may not realise are connected. Some teachers give the students sticky notes for their questions, but because they are adhesive, it is more difficult to sort the questions rapidly. For that reason, many teachers have found that a sheet of paper, cut into five strips provides the best compromise.

Getting students to write their questions down also helps them develop literacy skills, and teachers have reported that their students become better at asking questions. One secondary school maths teacher reported that she noticed a real change in the precision with which her students asked questions. She said that students used to say things like, "I can't do quadratics," and when the teacher asked what it was about quadratics they couldn't do, the students would respond by saying things like, "I can't do any of it." However, after some months of getting students to ask questions on strips of paper, she found that the students were more precise and focused, saying things like, "I can't do quadratics when there's a minus in front of the x squared."

Error Classification

This technique is useful when errors can be classified in a relatively straightforward way. For example, a teacher of Spanish collected final drafts of a piece of writing in Spanish; underlined, in pencil, errors in the text; and returned the work to the students. The students then had to classify the errors they had made (for example, tense, gender, pronouns, possessives). After determining the errors they had made and the areas in which they had made few errors, students identified a buddy with complementary strengths to help them correct their work.

What Did We Learn Today?

Other teachers have experimented with end-of-lesson reviews. One method that appears to be particularly effective is to form the class into groups five minutes before the end of the lesson and ask each group to produce a list of things they have learned during the lesson. Each group then reports one thing they have learned to the class. (The number of items in the list needs to be the same as the number of groups so that each group is guaranteed to have at least one thing on their list that has not been mentioned by the other groups.)

Student Reporter

An alternative to this is to have a student reporter lead the end-of-lesson discussion. At the beginning of the lesson (or at the end of the previous one), a student is appointed as a reporter for the lesson. The teacher then conducts the lesson as normal but finishes ten minutes before the scheduled end of the lesson. The student reporter then gives a summary of the main points of the lesson and tries to answer any remaining questions that students in the class may have (one teacher calls the selected student "The Captain" so the summary of the lesson is the "Captain's Log", as in *Star Trek*!). If she or he can't answer the questions, then the reporter asks members of the class to help out. Teachers who have tried this out have found that, although initially reluctant, pretty soon students are lining up to play the role of reporter; they see it as an opportunity to contribute to the learning of the whole class. One interesting approach is to ask the reporter, as he is observing the lesson, to make up questions to ask the class at the end. The teacher then uses the best of these questions for a "three-fourths of the way through a unit" test.

Preflight Checklist

This technique is particularly valuable when there are a number of clear requirements that submitted work has to satisfy. For example, science teachers routinely require laboratory reports to be structured in a standard way—for example, the report follows the sequence of question, hypothesis, method, results and conclusion; the report has a title that is underlined; the pages have margins; diagrams and graphs are drawn and labelled in pencil; and so on. Before a student can submit an assignment, it must be signed off by a buddy, who checks that all the required features are present. When the teacher marks the assignment, if any of the items on the preflight checklist are not up to standard, it is the buddy rather than the student submitting the assignment who is taken to task, thus creating a measure of accountability for the buddy to take the job seriously.

I-You-We Checklist

At the end of a group activity, each student records something about his or her own contributions, something about other individuals' contributions and an evaluation of the quality of the work of the group as a whole.

Reporter at Random

Many authors advocate assigning students roles, such as chair, timekeeper, facilitator, scribe and so on, when they are working collaboratively. This can be a good idea, but in general, it is a bad idea to assign the role of reporter at the outset. As soon as students know that someone else will have to report back, they can ease off, as the need for individual accountability has been weakened.

Group-Based Test Prep

When students are preparing for a test, one way to make reviewing more engaging is to organise them into groups of five or six and assign each student one aspect of the work to review. Each student is given a card on which details of a task are written, with suggestions for how it could be carried out. For instance, Dave Tuffin was preparing a year seven class for a test on the work they were just completing on plants. Each group was given six cards with the main topics they had covered (pollination, photosynthesis, starch test, seed dispersal, germination, flowers) and a brief description of the task. For example, the card for pollination read as follows:

> You have been asked to explain to the rest of the people in your group exactly what happens when an insect-pollinated plant reproduces. You should be able to describe where the pollen seed goes from and to, and how pollination results in the formation of a seed.

The following day, each member presents to the group. The rest of the group then responds to the presentation using coloured cups (see chapter 7) to traffic-light their responses: green means "better than I could have done"; yellow means "about the same as I would have done"; and red means "not as good as I would have done". After the voting, the group decides what needs to be added to the explanation to make it a good one.

If You've Learned It, Help Someone Who Hasn't

One objection of cooperative learning is that it holds back the able students. However, as discussed previously, if the students engaged in peer tutoring are providing elaborated explanations rather than just answers, then there is compelling evidence that both those who give and those who receive help will benefit.

Since cooperative learning cuts across the accepted demarcation of roles in classrooms, some teachers have found that high-achieving students have resisted peer tutoring because they claim that, as well as being held back, they are being asked to do the teacher's job for her. This appears to be particularly marked in mathematics, where there can be a great gulf between the highest achievers and the lowest achievers, particularly in terms of the speed with which assignments are completed. One tactic that is useful in countering this attitude is to make it clear that to be a good mathematician, getting the right answer isn't enough. One also has to communicate one's findings to other mathematicians. Being asked to explain how an answer was reached develops skills of mathematical communication that the high achiever needs to develop, even if he just wants to be a pure mathematician.

The attitude toward group work also depends on cultural norms. We have the saying "The squeaky wheel gets the grease." In Japan, there is a different saying: "*Deru kui wa utareru*," which, roughly translated, means, "The protruding nail gets hammered into place." The task of the Japanese teacher is to keep the class together; if one student has already understood the topic, then her task is to help other students who haven't.

As noted, the students who learn most in group work are those who give help and those who receive it, provided the help is in the form of elaborated explanations rather than just answers. If there is a large range of ability within a group, students in the middle can become disengaged spectators, watching the high achievers teach the low achievers. They don't need the help that the weakest students need, but they also aren't forced to articulate their thinking as the strongest students do when they teach others. Sometimes, therefore, it pays to have half-ability groups—weak with middle and middle with strong—so that as many students as possible are engaged in an activity that helps learning.

Another concern about this kind of approach often voiced by teachers is that it's not fair. One student gets everything right, and another makes many errors, but then the teacher or a peer shows the student what to do, and they are both at the same point. The fact that the first student got there more quickly than the second should somehow be recognised by giving him a higher score. But think about what happens when I take my car to the mechanic for a roadworthy check. My car, because it's been serviced recently, passes the first time. My neighbour's car fails, but at least he's told what's wrong. They don't just say, "Bring the car back when it's better." When he takes the car back with the problem fixed, he gets the same certificate I received. I don't get a bigger one, edged in gold, because I got it right the first time. The certificate simply shows that the car is satisfactory. In the same way, the primary purpose of assessment should not be to sort and rank and mark students. As we saw in chapter 5, we need to be careful to not create incentives for students to hand in low-quality work; the main purpose of assessment should be to provide information to the teacher to make real-time adjustments to his instruction in order to better meet the learning needs of his students.

Conclusion

In this chapter, we have seen that activating students as learning resources for one another produces tangible and substantial increases in students' learning. Every teacher I have ever met has acknowledged that you never really understand something until you try to teach it to someone else. And yet, despite this knowledge, we often fail to harness the power of peer tutoring and other forms of collaborative learning in our classrooms.

This chapter has presented a number of classroom techniques that can be used with students of almost any age and that can readily be incorporated into practice. Many of these techniques focus specifically on peer assessment, which, provided it is geared toward improvement rather than evaluation, can be especially powerful—students tend to be much more direct with each other than any teacher would dare to be. However, it is important to realise that peer assessment is also beneficial for the individual who gives help. When students provide feedback to each other, they are forced to internalise the learning intentions and success criteria but in the context of someone else's work, which is much less emotionally charged. Activating students as learning resources for one another can, therefore, be seen as a stepping-stone to students becoming owners of their own learning—the subject of the next chapter.

CHAPTER 7

Activating Students as Owners of Their Own Learning

In the introduction to his book *Guitar*, Dan Morgan (1965) wrote, "No one can teach you to play the guitar" (p. 1). This was rather puzzling, since the subtitle of the book is *The Book That Teaches You Everything You Need to Know About Playing the Guitar*. However, Morgan clarified by adding, "But they can help you learn." This is pretty obvious really. Whether learning to play a musical instrument, a sport or a whole range of other human endeavours, we intuitively grasp that teachers do not create learning; only learners create learning. And yet our classrooms seem to be based on the opposite principle—that if they try really hard, teachers can do the learning for the learners. This is only exacerbated by accountability regimes that mandate sanctions for teachers, for schools and for regions, but not for students.

This chapter reviews the research evidence on the impact of getting students more involved in their learning and shows that activating students as owners of their own learning can produce extraordinary improvements in their achievement. The chapter concludes with a number of practical techniques for classroom implementation.

Student Self-Assessment

To many, the phrase *student self-assessment* conjures up images of students giving themselves marks and diplomas, and the reaction is often predictable, including phrases like "lunatics running the asylum" or "fox guarding the henhouse". There is, in fact, evidence that students can assess themselves quite accurately for summative purposes (see, for example, Darrow, Johnson, Miller & Williamson, 2002) but only when the stakes are low. Whether or not students can assess themselves accurately for summative purposes is completely irrelevant to the topic of this chapter, which is whether students can develop sufficient insights into their own learning to improve it.

The answer is yes. The potential of student self-assessment for raising achievement was vividly demonstrated in a study of twenty-five primary school teachers in Portugal (Fontana & Fernandes, 1994). Over a twenty-week period, the teachers met for two hours each week, during which they were trained in the use of a structured approach to student self-assessment that involved both a prescriptive component and an exploratory component.

The prescriptive component took the form of a series of hierarchically organised activities, from which the teacher selected on the basis of diagnostic assessments of the students. For the exploratory component, each day at a set time, students organised and carried out individual plans of work, choosing tasks from a range offered by the teacher. The students had to evaluate their performance against their plans once each week. The progression within the exploratory component had two strands: over the twenty weeks, the tasks and areas in which the students worked took on the students' own ideas more and more, and the criteria that the students used to assess themselves became more objective and precise.

In the first two weeks, students chose from a set of carefully structured tasks and were then asked to assess their own performance. For the next four weeks, students constructed their own mathematical problems following the patterns of those used in weeks 1 and 2, and evaluated them as before, but this time, the students were required to identify any problems they had had and whether they had sought appropriate help from the teacher. Over the subsequent four weeks, students were given additional sets of learning objectives and again had to devise problems but were not given examples by the teacher. Finally, in the last ten weeks, students were allowed to set their own learning objectives, to construct relevant mathematical problems, to select appropriate apparatus, and to identify suitable self-assessments.

In order to evaluate the impact of the self-assessment activities on the students' progress, the achievement of the 354 students taught by the twenty-five study teachers was compared with that of 313 students taught by twenty teachers who had not been involved in the study in any way but were matched in terms of age, qualifications and experience, and had been using the same curriculum scheme for the same amount of time. To further ensure comparability, the twenty control teachers were provided with the same amount of in-service professional development but which was not focused on student self-assessment. A standardised mathematics test was administered to all 667 students at the beginning of the twenty-week study and again at the end. The scores of those taught by the control-group teachers went up by 7.8 points, while the scores of those taught by the teachers employing self-assessment rose by 15 points. In other words, through the development of their self-assessment skills, students managed to learn in twenty weeks what would otherwise have taken thirty-eight weeks to learn. Using self-assessment in these twenty-five classrooms had almost doubled the rate at which students were learning. How, exactly, attention to student self-assessment improves learning is not yet clear, but the most important element appears to be the notion of self-regulation.

Self-Regulated Learning

The basic idea of self-regulated learning is that the learner is able to coordinate cognitive resources, emotions and actions in the service of his learning goals (Boekaerts, 2006). Some (for example, Winne, 1996) have emphasised the cognitive aspects of this process—does the learner have the necessary knowledge, skills, strategies and so on to reach the goal? Others (for example, Corno, 2001) have pointed out that many students possess the necessary skills but do not use them in classrooms, which suggests that the problem is not a lack of skill but rather a lack of motivation or volition. Since the 1970s, there has been a great deal of research in these two broad areas—metacognition and motivation—which is summarised in the next two sections. Then these two threads will be woven together (Wigfield, Eccles & Rodriguez, 1998).

Metacognition

John Flavell (1976), widely credited with inventing the term, defined *metacognition* as follows:

> "Metacognition" refers to one's knowledge concerning one's own cognitive processes and products or anything related to them, e.g. the learning-relevant properties of information and data. For example I am engaging in metacognition (metamemory, metalearning, metaattention, metalanguage, or whatever) if I notice that I am having more trouble learning A than B; if it strikes me that I should double-check C before accepting it as a fact; if it occurs to me that I had better scrutinise each and every alternative in any multiple-choice type task situation before deciding which is the best one; if I sense that I had better make a note of D because I may forget it; if I think to ask someone about E to see if I have it right. In any kind of cognitive transaction with the human or nonhuman environment, a variety of information processing activities may go on. Metacognition refers, among other things, to the active monitoring and consequent regulation and orchestration of these processes in relation to the cognitive objects or data on which they bear, usually in the service of some concrete goal or objective. (p. 232)

Metacognition, therefore, includes knowing what one knows (*metacognitive knowledge*), what one can do (*metacognitive skills*), and what one knows about one's own cognitive abilities (*metacognitive experience*). The research shows clearly that "the most effective learners are self-regulating" (Butler & Winne, 1995, p. 245) and, more importantly, that training students in metacognition raises their performance (for example, Lodico, Ghatala, Levin, Pressley & Bell, 1983) and allows them to generalise what they have learned to novel situations (Hacker, Dunlosky & Graesser, 1998). However, these skills will be useful only if students are motivated to use them.

Motivation

Most people are familiar with the distinction between intrinsic and extrinsic motivation: whether the motivation for doing something comes from the fact that it is inherently interesting or enjoyable or because it will lead to some other valued outcome (Ryan & Deci, 2000). If individuals undertake only those things that are inherently interesting or enjoyable, then they are unlikely to learn to read, write or play a musical instrument. We are generally motivated to learn these things because we value the consequence, whether it is avoiding punishment such as that for not doing homework or reaching some external goal we have set for ourselves such as learning to drive or learning how to play a favourite song on the guitar.

In much writing about motivation in school, motivation is treated rather like a substance in students' brains. Some students have a lot of it, and others don't. When students fail to learn, we blame their lack of motivation. At the other extreme, there are those who believe that it is the teacher's job to motivate the students. If the students don't learn, it is because the teacher was not a sufficiently good motivator, so the cause of the failure to learn is the teacher.

There is another way to think about motivation—not as a cause but as a *consequence* of achievement. This way of thinking is particularly marked in the work of Mihaly Csikszentmihalyi, a psychologist at the University of Chicago. In his book *Flow: The Psychology of Optimal Experience*, Csikszentmihalyi (1990) described a number of situations in which individuals became completely absorbed in the activities in which they were engaged:

> A dancer describes how it feels when a performance is going well: "Your concentration is very complete. Your mind isn't wandering, you are not thinking of something else; you are totally involved in what you are doing. . . . Your energy is flowing very smoothly. You feel relaxed, comfortable and energetic."

> A rock climber describes how it feels when he is scaling a mountain: "You are so involved in what you are doing [that] you aren't thinking of yourself as separate from the immediate activity. . . . You don't see yourself as separate from what you are doing."

> A mother who enjoys the time spent with her small daughter: "Her reading is the one thing she's really into, and we read together. She reads to me and I read to her, and that's a time

when I sort of lose touch with the rest of the world, I'm totally absorbed in what I'm doing."

A chess player tells of playing in a tournament: " . . . the concentration is like breathing—you never think of it. The roof could fall in and, if it missed you, you would be unaware of it." (pp. 53–54)

Csikszentmihalyi described this sense of being completely absorbed in an activity "flow". This sense of flow can arise because of one's intrinsic interest in a task, as with the mother reading to her daughter, but can also arise through a match between one's capability and the challenge of the task. When the level of challenge is low and the level of capability is high, the result is often boredom. When the level of challenge is high and the level of capability is low, the result is generally anxiety. When both are low, the result is apathy. However, when both capability and challenge are high, the result is "flow".

This way of thinking about motivation is radical because it does not locate "the problem" in the teacher or the learner but in the match between challenge and capability. In the traditional view of motivation, if the student is not motivated, it is the fault either of the teacher or of the student. But if we see motivation not as a cause but as an outcome, an emergent property of getting the match between challenge and capability right, then if the student isn't motivated, that's just a signal that the teacher and the learner need to try something different.

However, it will not be enough that an activity is absorbing if the cost of engaging in the task is seen by the student as being too high, whether this is in terms of the opportunity cost that attempting a task might take or negative consequences such as the risk to one's self-image if unsuccessful (Eccles et al., 1983). The goals that students actually pursue in classrooms will depend on complex trade-offs between cost and benefit.

We know that students are more motivated to reach goals that are specific, are within reach, and offer some degree of challenge (Bandura, 1986; Schunk, 1991), but when the goals seem out of reach, students may give up on increasing competence and instead avoid harm, by either focusing on lower-level goals they know they can reach or avoiding failing altogether by disengaging from the task, as we saw in chapter 5. It might be assumed from this that competition is unhelpful, but focusing on increasing competence within teams to compete against other teams has been found to increase student achievement in maths, provided the competition was focused on relative improvement among the groups (Linnenbrink, 2005).

It is also worth noting that while students' motivation and their belief in their ability to carry their plans through to successful completion—what Albert Bandura (1997) termed *self-efficacy*—tend to decline as students go through school, what the teacher does can make a real difference. A study of 1571 students in eighty-four mathematics classrooms from years five to twelve found that students provided with positive constructive feedback by their teachers were more likely to focus on learning rather than performance (Deevers, 2006).

Integrating Motivational and Cognitive Perspectives

This discussion may appear to have brought us a long distance from classroom formative assessment, but fulfilling the potential of formative assessment requires that we recognise that assessment is a two-edged sword. Assessment can improve instruction, but it can also impact the learner's willingness, desire and capacity to learn (Harlen & Deakin Crick, 2002). Although we don't yet know everything about the most effective learning environments, the existing research on cognition and motivation provides clear and strong evidence that activating students as owners of their own learning is an essential component.

When students are invited to participate in a learning activity, they use three sources of information to decide what they are going to do:

1. Their perceptions of the task and its context (for example, school, class and so on)

2. Their knowledge about the task and what it will take to be successful

3. Their motivational beliefs, including their interest and whether they think they know enough to succeed

The student then weighs the information and begins to channel energy along one of two pathways, focusing on either growth or well-being. This, however, is dynamic and can change rapidly. For example, after giving some attention to well-being, a student may find a way to lower the threat to self-image, thus allowing a shift of energy and attention back to the growth pathway.

The motivational and cognitive perspectives on self-regulated learning can be brought together within the dual-processing model developed by Monique Boekaerts (1993). The dual-processing model suggests that the most important thing is the creation of learning environments that encourage students to activate the growth rather than the well-being pathway. We cannot possibly anticipate all the factors that a student may take into account in deciding whether to pursue growth rather than well-being, but there are a number of things that can be done to tip the scales in the right direction:

1. Share learning goals with students so that they are able to monitor their own progress toward them.

2. Promote the belief that ability is incremental rather than fixed; when students think they can't get smarter, they are likely to devote their energy to avoiding failure.

3. Make it more difficult for students to compare themselves with others in terms of achievement.

4. Provide feedback that contains a recipe for future action rather than a review of past failures (a medical rather than a postmortem).

5. Use every opportunity to transfer executive control of the learning from the teacher to the students to support their development as autonomous learners.

And if you figure out a way to do all that, please let me know. The fact that we know what needs to be done is not the same as doing it. Continuously developing one's teaching is extraordinarily difficult. The good news is that you don't need to start from scratch but build on the achievements of other teachers who have already developed techniques, such as those in the next section.

Practical Techniques

There is no doubt that activating students as owners of their own learning produces substantial increases in learning, but it is not a quick fix. Many teachers have found that students' first attempts at self-assessment are usually neither insightful nor useful. One teacher said, "It's like making pancakes; you usually end up throwing the first one away." It is also a difficult course to steer. One project on Records of Achievement in England encouraged students to compile personal statements of their own achievements to show potential employers (Andrews, 1988). But when students of African heritage included items about their interest in break dancing or Rastafarianism in their personal statements, they were told to remove these items as they would not be welcomed by employers; the need for the personal statements to show the student in the best possible light to an employer was seen by teachers as incompatible with the students putting forward their true sense of themselves.

On a more prosaic level, a homeroom teacher was addressing some behaviour problems that had arisen in a middle years class's maths lessons. The homeroom teacher decided to try to help the maths teacher by getting the students to do a self-assessment of their own performance and asked each student to complete the sentence "I would learn better in maths lessons if . . ." One girl thought about this for quite a while, and in the end, she wrote, "I would learn better in maths lessons if I had a better maths teacher." I have been in her maths classroom, and she has a point. However, when the homeroom teacher saw what the student had written, she told the student that this was not acceptable, so the student went back to her seat and wrote, "I would learn better in maths lessons if I brought the right equipment to school, paid attention in class and remembered to do my homework." Originally, the student thought that her homeroom teacher really wanted her to engage in working on what would improve her learning of maths, but the homeroom teacher hadn't provided sufficient guidance about what was and was not up for negotiation. More importantly, the self-assessment activity had not been framed sufficiently well to ensure that the students focused on things that were within their control. In such cases, the students end up playing a game of "guess what's in the teacher's head" and there is little, or no, worthwhile learning. As we will see, self-assessment can be uncomfortable for both student and teacher, but the benefits are great, and once teachers get used to involving the students in their own learning, it is almost impossible to go back.

Many of the techniques described in chapter 6 can be adapted for self-assessment, but following are some techniques that are specifically designed to encourage students to reflect upon their own learning.

Traffic Lights

Many teachers use "traffic lights" to activate students as owners of their own learning. At the beginning of the lesson, the teacher shares the learning intentions and any associated success criteria with the students, and at the end of the period, the students have to assess the extent to which they have achieved the intended learning by placing a coloured circle against the learning intention that they wrote in their notebooks at the start of the lesson. Green indicates confidence that the intended learning has been achieved. Yellow indicates either ambivalence about the extent to which the intended learning has been achieved or that the objectives have been partially met. Red indicates that the student believes that he or she has not learned what was intended. The problem is that this is a self-report, and as noted earlier, self-reports are not particularly reliable. One teacher addressed this by saying to the class, "Reds over here with me; greens help the yellows; yellows make sure the greens understand this as well as they think they do." By changing the meaning of green from "I feel confident" to "I am now ready to teach this to someone else," the teacher made it much less likely that students would signal green just because they wanted to look good.

Traffic lights can also be used for test preparation. One teacher had been looking at how her students prepared for tests and was concerned to see that many of her students seemed to employ as their primary strategy flipping through the pages of their notebooks, presumably hoping that some of it would stick. She was particularly surprised to see that many students spent as much time reviewing the things that they were confident about as they did reviewing things they had not learned. To improve the quality of preparation, the teacher encouraged students to place a coloured dot in the top corner of each page to signal the students' confidence with the material. When preparing for the test, students could then skip over the material they had flagged as green and concentrate on those areas in which they were less confident. While such an approach depends on the accuracy of the students' judgments, which are, after all, self-reports, the fact that the only audience for this self-assessment is the student himself increases the likelihood that he will be honest.

Red/Green Disks

A secondary school algebra teacher had been using traffic lights for a while and started thinking about how she could get more real-time information. She gave each student in the class a CD-sized disk, green on one side and red on the other. At the beginning of the period, the green side faced up, but, as the lesson progressed, if students wanted to signal that they thought the teacher was going too fast, they flipped the disk over to red. She found that students who hadn't asked a single question that year in class were willing to flip the disk over to red to show that they were getting confused.

A few weeks later, something rather remarkable occurred. Using an overhead projector, the teacher was showing a class of students who were taking Algebra I for the second time how to solve equations. She got so wrapped up in what she was doing that she forgot to check for any red disks. A student at the back of the class had flipped her disk over to red a few minutes earlier and was getting more and more frustrated that the teacher had not checked for red disks. She looked at her two friends seated on either side, and realising that they didn't understand what was going on either, she grabbed their two disks and waved all three disks in the air to flag the teacher to slow down. When I first heard this story, I thought, this must have been an extraordinarily confident student, but over time, as more and more teachers have used these techniques, more and more stories of this kind have emerged. When teachers open the channels of communication with the students, the students will use them.

Sometimes the honesty of students can be disarming—even scary. Dave Tuffin, a science teacher, was teaching a lesson to a year seven class on a hot summer afternoon. He described it as "one of those lessons where you know it's not working but you can't stop yourself"—an experience that will be familiar to every teacher. He was trying to get more animated in order to wake up the class, but in reality, he was in a hole, and still digging. Then one student raised his hand and said, "Sir, this isn't working, is it?" Afterward Dave described his feelings, saying that a year earlier he would have been really angry with the student for embarrassing him in that way. But for months, he had been trying to get the students to take more responsibility for their own learning, and so he said, "You're right. What shall we do?" Not one student suggested having a recess or giving up on the science. Instead, the whole class had a mature conversation about how to improve their learning of the lesson. Perhaps the most important thing about this story is the reaction of the teacher. We saw in Chapter 5 how important it is to get the egos of the students out of the learning situation, but this story shows how important it is to get the teacher's ego out of the classroom, too. The student was not trying to embarrass Dave. He was throwing him a life-line, and Dave had the grace to realise this and grab it.

Coloured Cups

Another teacher had tried the red/green disks but found that the disks were difficult to see clearly from the front of her classroom due to the fluorescent lighting. So she went to a party shop and bought coloured cups, in red, yellow and green. In her classroom, each student is given one of each of the coloured cups, and the lesson begins with the green cup showing. If the student wants to signal that the teacher is going too fast, then the student shows the yellow cup, and if a student wants to ask a question, then the red cup is displayed. Why would any student show red? Because in this classroom, the rule is that as soon as one student shows red, the teacher uses the icy pole sticks to pick another student at random, and the selected student has to go to the front of the classroom to answer the question being posed by the student who showed red. The teacher describes this as converting her classroom into one gigantic game of chicken.

This technique neatly encapsulates two key components of effective formative assessment—engagement and contingency. If a student is showing yellow or green, he can be called upon to explain the work to someone else, which requires the students to be monitoring their own learning and, therefore, engaged. And the flow of information from the students about the pace of instruction helps the teacher make adjustments to better meet the students' learning needs.

Learning Portfolios

Many schools encourage students to keep portfolios of their work, but too often, these are maintained in the same way as an artist's portfolio—to display the latest and best. In her portfolio, an artist might have something in gouache, something in acrylic, something in watercolour, something in oil and something in charcoal. If the artist produces a new work in, say, gouache that she considers to be better than what is already in the portfolio, then she will replace the old gouache piece with the new one. Focusing on the latest and best in this way creates what might be termed a "performance portfolio", which supports summative assessment well but tends to obscure the learning journey.

For an incremental view of ability, a "learning portfolio" is far more useful. When better work is done, it is added to the portfolio rather than replacing earlier work to allow students to review their learning journeys. By looking back at earlier samples of their persuasive writing, for example, students can see what has developed, which has two immediate benefits. The first is that by seeing what has improved and thus identifying a trajectory of development, the student is likely to be able to see how further improvement might be possible. The second is that by focusing on improvement, the student is more likely to see ability as incremental rather than fixed, which, as we saw in chapter 5, is a key characteristic of the most effective learners.

Students can start developing such learning portfolios at a very young age. One kindergarten teacher gets her students to paint a self-portrait each month, and these are placed in the student's learning portfolio. In January, the students review their four self-portraits from September, October, November and December and are asked to reflect on what they think has gotten better in their painting. In discussion with her teacher, one girl decided that the most salient feature was "my arms don't come out of my head anymore." This student may not be the best painter in the class, but she knows that with continued effort, she will improve.

Learning Logs

One technique that teachers have found useful as a way of getting students to reflect on their learning is to ask students to complete a learning log at the end of a lesson. Of course, there is nothing new in this, but some teachers have found a slight variant on the usual method useful. Instead of providing responses to one or two self-assessment questions provided by the teacher, students are invited to respond to no more than three of the following prompts:

- Today I learned . . .
- I was surprised by . . .
- The most useful thing I will take from this lesson is . . .
- I was interested in . . .
- What I liked most about this lesson was . . .
- One thing I'm not sure about is . . .
- The main thing I want to find out more about is . . .

- After this session, I feel . . .
- I might have gotten more from this lesson if . . .

Getting students to choose which three of these statements they respond to seems to encourage a more thoughtful approach to the process of reflecting on their learning.

Conclusion

Teachers have a crucial role to play in designing the situations in which learning takes place, but only learners create learning. Therefore, it is not surprising that the better learners are able to manage their learning, the better they learn. All students can improve how they manage learning processes and become owners of their own learning. However, this is not an easy process. Reflecting critically on one's own learning is emotionally charged, which is why developing such skills takes time, especially with students who are accustomed to failure.

This chapter has provided research evidence along with a number of practical techniques that teachers have used to increase the engagement of their students and their own responsiveness to their students' needs. In the epilogue, the main themes of this book are reviewed, concluding with a few words of advice for teachers in taking the ideas presented in this book into their own classrooms.

Epilogue

Every generation believes it is witnessing unprecedented change, in society, in the world of work, and in the demands that are made of people. However, there are good reasons to believe that this time, it really is different. As we saw in chapter 1, as many as 50 million American jobs are at risk of being offshored by 2025. Some of these are low-skill jobs, but many are not. At the time of this writing, America is still (just) the largest manufacturer in the world, although China will overtake the US soon if it has not already done so. But the average American worker is three to four times as productive as the average Chinese worker (United Nations Statistics Division, 2010), not because they work with more expensive equipment, but because of intangibles such as ways of organising work, the intellectual property being used and so on (Kling & Schulz, 2009).

America became the world's manufacturer in the second half of the 20th century because, between 1910 and 1940, it made extraordinary investments in mass public education for students up to the age of eighteen, at a time when most other equally developed economies thought that education beyond the age of fifteen would be wasted on those not going on to higher education (Goldin & Katz, 2008). This investment created both a skilled workforce and a set of consumers who were well enough educated to be able to adopt the new technology (Bhidé, 2008).

The important feature of the investment that was made in educating America's youngsters between 1910 and 1940 was that it did not try to predict the future, and it was successful precisely for that reason. The education provided was general education, not vocational training targeted at specific jobs. Indications suggest that it is more, and better, *general* education for more of the population that will guarantee America's future prosperity.

If we looked at previous attempts to improve reading and mathematics, we would probably get very depressed. The data from the National Assessment of Educational Progress (Rampey, Dion & Donahue, 2009) show that while there have been some improvements in the performance of nine- and thirteen-year-olds, the reading and maths levels of seventeen-year-olds are the same as they were in the early 1970s. However, as we saw in chapter 1, the failure to improve education arises primarily from a failure to understand the importance of teacher quality.

During the twentieth century, most policies for educational improvement assumed that all teachers were more or less the same. Now we understand that the quality of the teacher is the single most important determinant of how much students learn, and in the classrooms of the most effective teachers, students from disadvantaged backgrounds learn as much as those from advantaged backgrounds. The impact of teacher quality is profound.

The study from Harvard University mentioned in chapter 1 showed that the impact of having an outstanding teacher in kindergarten can be detected in the annual salaries of those students thirty years later (Chetty et al., 2010). There is now widespread agreement about the importance of teacher quality—indeed, it appears that differences in the quality of schools are almost entirely accounted for by differences in the quality of the teachers at the schools. To raise student achievement, we have to improve teacher quality.

Given the failure of most attempts to improve teacher performance, it is hardly surprising that many economists of education have suggested that the only way to improve teacher quality is through deselecting the least effective teachers and replacing them with better ones (Hanushek, 2010). However, such a change will take thirty years to work through the system, by which time it will be too late. Therefore, while we should, of course, seek to ensure that the best people are attracted to and remain in teaching, we must also seek to improve the performance of existing teachers, through professional development focused on what the research shows as making the biggest difference to students.

In chapter 2, we saw that the research evidence available indicates that when formative assessment practices are integrated into the minute-to-minute and day-by-day classroom activities of teachers, substantial increases in student achievement—of the order of a 70 to 80 per cent increase in the speed of learning—are possible, even when outcomes are measured with externally mandated standardised tests. Moreover, these changes are not expensive to produce; classroom formative assessment is approximately twenty times as cost effective in raising achievement as class-size reduction. The currently available evidence suggests that there is nothing else remotely affordable that is likely to have such a large effect.

Chapters 3 to 7 reviewed the five key strategies of classroom formative assessment:

1. Clarifying, sharing and understanding learning intentions and criteria for success

2. Engineering effective classroom discussions, activities and learning tasks that elicit evidence of learning

3. Providing feedback that moves learning forward

4. Activating learners as instructional resources for one another

5. Activating learners as owners of their own learning

For each of these strategies, evidence of its impact on student learning was presented, and a number of practical classroom techniques for implementing the strategy were provided. Each of the techniques requires little in the way of technology and can be easily adapted to use in the teaching of any subject, for any age range.

Some of the techniques are relatively new, but most are not. They have been used by the best teachers for tens, if not hundreds, of years. It is not the techniques that are new—rather, it is the framework provided by classroom formative assessment that shows how they fit together and the evidence that shows the impact of such techniques on student achievement.

The problem with being provided with so many techniques is that, as Barry Schwartz (2003) has pointed out in *The Paradox of Choice*, too much choice can be paralysing—and dangerous. When teachers try to change more than two or three things about their teaching at the same time, the typical result is that their teaching deteriorates and they go back to doing what they were doing before. My advice is that each teacher chooses one or two of the techniques in this book and tries them out in the classroom. If they appear to be effective, then the goal should be to practise them until they become second nature. If they are not effective, then they can be modified or the teacher can try another technique. None of these techniques are likely to work for all teachers, but all teachers will, I believe, find something here that will work for them.

In her book *A Return to Love*, Marianne Williamson (1992) writes, "Our deepest fear is not that we are inadequate. Our deepest fear is that we are powerful beyond measure" (p. 190). We now know that the teacher is the most powerful influence on how much a student learns and that teachers can continue to make significant improvements in their practice throughout their entire careers. If all teachers accept the need to improve practice, not because they are not good enough, but because they can be even better, and focus on the things that make the biggest difference to their students, according to the research, we *will* be able to prepare our students to thrive in the impossibly complex, unpredictable world of the 21st century.

List of Techniques

References and Resources

Adey, P. S., Fairbrother, R. W., Wiliam, D., Johnson, B. & Jones, C. (1999). *A review of research related to learning styles and strategies*. London: King's College London Centre for the Advancement of Thinking.

Allal, L. & Lopez, L. M. (2005). Formative assessment of learning: A review of publications in French. In J. Looney (Ed.), *Formative assessment: Improving learning in secondary classrooms* (pp. 241–264). Paris: Organisation for Economic Co-operation and Development.

Andrews, S. (1988). *Records of achievement: R. A. Essex leaves school (sixty school/college leavers speak about involvement in Records of Achievement)*. London: The Industrial Society.

Antil, L. R., Jenkins, J. R., Wayne, S. K. & Vadasy, P. F. (1998). Cooperative learning: Prevalence, conceptualization and the relation between research and practice. *American Educational Research Journal, 35*(3), 419–454.

Arter, J. A. & McTighe, J. (2001, 2005). *Scoring rubrics in the classroom*. Melbourne, Victoria: Hawker Brownlow Education.

Ausubel, D. P. (1968). *Educational psychology: A cognitive view*. New York: Holt, Rinehart and Winston.

Autor, D. H., Levy, F. & Murnane, R. J. (2003). The skill content of recent technological change: An empirical exploration. *Quarterly Journal of Economics, 118*(4), 1279–1333.

Babcock, J., Babcock, P., Buhler, J., Cady, J., Cogan, L. S., Houang, R. T. et al. (2010). *Breaking the cycle: An international comparison of U.S. mathematics teacher preparation*. East Lansing: Michigan State University Center for Research in Mathematics and Science Education.

Bacolod, M. P. (2007). Do alternative opportunities matter? The role of female labor markets in the decline of teacher supply and teacher quality 1940–1990. *Review of Economics and Statistics, 89*(4), 737–751.

Bandura, A. (1986). *Social foundations of thought and action: A social cognitive theory*. Englewood Cliffs, NJ: Prentice Hall.

Bandura, A. (1997). *Self-efficacy: The exercise of control*. New York: Freeman.

Bangert-Drowns, R. L., Kulik, J. A. & Kulik, C.-L. C. (1991). Effects of frequent classroom testing. *Journal of Educational Research, 85*(2), 89–99.

Bangert-Drowns, R. L., Kulik, C.-L. C., Kulik, J. A. & Morgan, M. (1991). The instructional effect of feedback in test-like events. *Review of Educational Research, 61*(2), 213–238.

Barber, M. & Mourshed, M. (2007). *How the world's best-performing school systems come out on top.* London: McKinsey.

Barry, D. (Series Producer), & Hardy, E. (Executive Producer). (2010). *The classroom experiment* [Television series]. London: British Broadcasting Corporation.

Bennett, R. E. (2009). *A critical look at the meaning and basis of formative assessment* (ETS Research Memorandum No. RM-09–06). Princeton, NJ: Educational Testing Service.

Bernstein, B. (1970). Education cannot compensate for society. *New Society, 15*(387), 344–347.

Bhidé, A. V. (2008). *The venturesome economy: How innovation sustains prosperity in a more connected world.* Princeton, NJ: Princeton University Press.

Black, H. (1986). Assessment for learning. In D. L. Nuttall (Ed.), *Assessing educational achievement* (pp. 7–18). London: Falmer Press.

Black, P. & Harrison, C. (2002). *Science inside the black box: Assessment for learning in the science classroom.* London: King's College London Department of Education and Professional Studies.

Black, P., Harrison, C., Lee, C., Marshall, B. & Wiliam, D. (2003). *Assessment for learning: Putting it into practice.* Berkshire, England: Open University Press.

Black, P., Harrison, C., Lee, C., Marshall, B. & Wiliam, D. (2004). Working inside the black box: Assessment for learning in the classroom. *Phi Delta Kappan, 86*(1), 8–21.

Black, P. J. & Wiliam, D. (1998a). Assessment and classroom learning. *Assessment in Education: Principles, Policy & Practice, 5*(1), 7–73.

Black, P. J. & Wiliam, D. (1998b). *Inside the black box: Raising standards through classroom assessment.* London: King's College London School of Education.

Black, P. J. & Wiliam, D. (2009). Developing the theory of formative assessment. *Educational Assessment, Evaluation and Accountability, 21*(1), 5–31.

Blatchford, P., Basset, P., Brown, P., Martin, C., Russell, A. & Webster, R. (2009). *Deployment and impact of support staff in schools: Characteristics, working conditions and job satisfaction of support staff in schools (strand 1, waves 1–3 in 2004, 2006 and 2008)* (Research Report No. DCSF-RR154). London: Department for Children, Schools and Families.

Blinder, A. (2010). *How many U.S. jobs might be offshorable?* Princeton, NJ: Princeton University Center for Economic Policy Studies.

Bloom, B. S. (1969). Some theoretical issues relating to educational evaluation. In H. G. Richey & R. W. Tyler (Eds.), *Educational evaluation: New roles, new means, pt. 2* (Vol. 68, pp. 26–50). Chicago: University of Chicago Press.

Boaler, J. (2002). *Experiencing school mathematics: Traditional and reform approaches to teaching and their impact on student learning.* Mahwah, NJ: Erlbaum.

Boekaerts, M. (1993). Being concerned with well being and with learning. *Educational Psychologist, 28*(2), 149–167.

Boekaerts, M. (2006). Self-regulation and effort investment. In K. A. Renninger & I. E. Sigel (Eds.), *Handbook of child psychology: Vol. 4. Child psychology in practice* (6th ed., pp. 345–377). New York: Wiley.

Böhlmark, A. & Lindahl, M. (2008). *Does school privatization improve educational achievement? Evidence from Sweden's voucher reform.* Bonn, Germany: Forschungsinstitut zur Zukunft der Arbeit (Institute for the Study of Labour).

Bondy, F. (1999, January 13). Out of this world in redefining greatness, Michael Jordan made a lasting impact on an entire generation. *New York Daily News*, p. 2.

Boulet, M. M., Simard, G. & De Melo, D. (1990). Formative evaluation effects on learning music. *Journal of Educational Research, 84*(2), 119–125.

Boykin, A. W., Coleman, S. T., Lilja, A. & Tyler, K. M. (2004). *Building on children's cultural assets in simulated classroom performance environments: Research vistas in the communal learning paradigm* (Report No. 68). Baltimore: Center for Research on the Education of Students Placed at Risk.

Boykin, A. W., Lilja, A. & Tyler, K. M. (2004). The influence of communal vs. individual learning context on the academic performance in social studies of grade 4–5 African-Americans. *Learning Environments Research, 7*(3), 227–244.

Boyle, G. J. (1995). Myers-Briggs Type Indicator (MBTI): Some psychometric limitations. *Australian Psychologist, 30*(1), 71–74.

Broadfoot, P. M., Daugherty, R., Gardner, J., Gipps, C. V., Harlen, W., James, M. et al. (1999). *Assessment for learning: Beyond the black box.* Cambridge, England: University of Cambridge School of Education.

Brookhart, S. M. (2004). Classroom assessment: Tensions and intersections in theory and practice. *Teachers College Record, 106*(3), 429–458.

Brookhart, S. M. (2007). Expanding views about formative classroom assessment:

A review of the literature. In J. H. McMillan (Ed.), *Formative classroom assessment: Theory into practice* (pp. 43–62). New York: Teachers College Press.

Brophy, J. (1981). Teacher praise: A functional analysis. *Review of Educational Research, 51*(1), 5–32.

Brousseau, G. (1984). The crucial role of the didactical contract in the analysis and construction of situations in teaching and learning mathematics (G. Seib, Trans.). In H.-G. Steiner (Ed.), *Theory of mathematics education: ICME 5 topic area and miniconference* (Vol. 54, pp. 110–119). Bielefeld, Germany: Institut für Didaktik der Mathematik der Universität Bielefeld.

Brown, A. L. & Campione, J. C. (1996). Psychological theory and the design of innovative learning environments: On procedures, principles, and systems. In L. Schauble & R. Glaser (Eds.), *Innovations in learning: New environments for education* (pp. 291–292). Hillsdale, NJ: Erlbaum.

Brown, G. & Wragg, E. C. (1993). *Questioning.* London: Routledge.

Bruer, J. T. (1997). Education and the brain: A bridge too far. *Educational Research, 26*(8), 4–16.

Bruer, J. T. (1999). In search of . . . brain-based education. *Phi Delta Kappan, 80*(9), 648–657.

Buddin, R., & Zamarro, G. (2009). Teacher qualifications and student achievement in urban elementary schools. *Journal of Urban Economics, 66*(2), 103–115.

Bursten, L. (Ed.). (1992). *The IEA study of mathematics III: Student growth and classroom processes.* Oxford, England: Pergamon Press.

Burute, N. & Jankharia, B. (2009). Teleradiology: The Indian perspective. *Indian Journal of Radiological Imaging, 19*(1), 16–18.

Butler, D. L. & Winne, P. H. (1995). Feedback and self-regulated learning: A theoretical synthesis. *Review of Educational Research, 65*(3), 245–281.

Butler, R. (1987). Task-involving and ego-involving properties of evaluation: Effects of different feedback conditions on motivational perceptions, interest and performance. *Journal of Educational Psychology, 79*(4), 474–482.

Butler, R. (1988). Enhancing and undermining intrinsic motivation; the effects of task-involving and ego-involving evaluation on interest and performance. *British Journal of Educational Psychology, 58*, 1–14.

Carnoy, M., Jacobsen, R., Mishel, L. & Rothstein, R. (2005). *The charter school dust-up: Examining the evidence on enrollment and achievement.* Washington, DC: Economic Policy Institute.

Carpenter, T. P., Fennema, E., Peterson, P. L., Chiang, C. P. & Loef, M. (1989).

Using knowledge of children's mathematics thinking in classroom teaching: An experimental study. *American Educational Research Journal, 26*(4), 499–531.

Center for Research on Education Outcomes. (2009). *Multiple choice: Charter school performance in 16 states.* Stanford, CA: Author.

Chetty, R., Friedman, J. N., Hilger, N., Saez, E., Schanzenbach, D. & Yagan, D. (2010). *How does your kindergarten classroom affect your earnings? Evidence from project STAR.* Cambridge, MA: Harvard Graduate School of Education.

Clarke, S. (2005). *Formative assessment in the secondary classroom.* London: Hodder & Stoughton.

Claxton, G. L. (1995). What kind of learning does self-assessment drive? Developing a "nose" for quality: Comments on Klenowski. *Assessment in Education: Principles, Policy and Practice, 2*(3), 339–343.

Clymer, J. B. & Wiliam, D. (2006/2007). Improving the way we grade science. *Educational Leadership, 64*(4), 36–42.

Cohen, E. G. (1994). Restructuring the classroom: Conditions for productive small groups. *Review of Educational Research, 64*(1), 1–35.

Committee on the Study of Teacher Preparation Programs in the United States. (2010). *Preparing teachers: Building evidence for sound policy.* Washington, DC: National Research Council.

Corno, L. (2001). Volitional aspects of self-regulated learning. In B. J. Zimmerman & D. H. Schunk (Eds.), *Self-regulated learning and academic achievement: Theoretical perspectives* (2nd ed., pp. 191–225). Hillsdale, NJ: Erlbaum.

Cowie, B., & Bell, B. (1999). A model of formative assessment in science education. *Assessment in Education: Principles, Policy and Practice, 6*(1), 32–42.

Crooks, T. J. (1988). The impact of classroom evaluation practices on students. *Review of Educational Research, 58*(4), 438–481.

Csikszentmihalyi, M. (1990). *Flow: The psychology of optimal experience.* New York: Harper & Row.

Cuban, L. (2002). *Oversold and underused: Computers in the classroom.* Cambridge, MA: Harvard University Press.

Darling-Hammond, L., Holtzman, D. J., Gatlin, S. J. & Vasquez Heilig, J. (2005). Does teacher preparation matter? Evidence about teacher certification, Teach for America, and teacher effectiveness. *Education Policy Analysis Archives, 13*(42).

Darrow, A.-A., Johnson, C. M., Miller, A. M. & Williamson, P. (2002). Can students accurately assess themselves? Predictive validity of student self-reports. *Applications of Research in Music Education, 20*(2), 8–11.

Davies, P., Durbin, C., Clarke, J. & Dale, J. (2004). Developing students' conceptions of quality in geography. *Curriculum Journal, 15*(1), 19–34.

Davis, B. (1997). Listening for differences: An evolving conception of mathematics teaching. *Journal for Research in Mathematics Education, 28*(3), 355–376.

Dawes, L., Mercer, N. & Wegerif, R. (2000). *Thinking together: A programme of activities for developing speaking, listening and thinking skills for children aged 8–11.* Birmingham, England: Imaginative Minds.

Day, J. D. & Cordón, L. A. (1993). Static and dynamic measures of ability: An experimental comparison. *Journal of Educational Psychology, 85*(1), 76–82.

Deevers, M. (2006, April). *Linking classroom assessment practices with student motivation in mathematics.* Paper presented at the annual meeting of the American Educational Research Association, San Francisco, CA.

Dempster, F. N. (1991). Synthesis of research on reviews and tests. *Educational Leadership, 48*(7), 71–76.

Denvir, B. & Brown, M. L. (1986a). Understanding of number concepts in low-attaining 7-9 year olds: Part I. Development of descriptive framework and diagnostic instrument. *Educational Studies in Mathematics, 17*(1), 15–36.

Denvir, B. & Brown, M. L. (1986b). Understanding of number concepts in low-attaining 7-9 year olds: Part II. The teaching studies. *Educational Studies in Mathematics, 17*(2), 143–164.

Dillon, J. T. (1988). *Questioning and teaching: A manual of practice.* London: Croom Helm.

Dressel, P. (1957, Winter). Grades: One more tilt at the windmill. *Basic College Quarterly* (Michigan State University), 6.

Dweck, C. S. (1975). The role of expectations and attributions in the alleviation of learned helplessness. *Journal of Personality and Social Psychology, 31*(4), 674–685.

Dweck, C. S. (2000). *Self-theories: Their role in motivation, personality and development.* Philadelphia: Psychology Press.

Dweck, C. S. (2006). *Mindset: The new psychology of success.* New York: Random House.

Eccles, J. S., Adler, T. F., Futterman, R., Goff, S. B., Kaczala, C. M., Meece, J. L. et al. (1983). Expectancies, values, and academic behaviors. In J. T. Spence (Ed.), *Achievement and achievement motivation* (pp. 75–146). San Francisco: Freeman.

Economic Policy Institute. (2010). *Wage and compensation trends: Real hourly wage for all by education, 1973–2007.* Accessed at www.epi.org/page/-/datazone 2008/wage%20comp%20trends/wagebyed_a.xls on May 28, 2010.

Educational Testing Service. (2002). *Standards for quality and fairness.* Princeton, NJ: Author.

Elawar, M. C. & Corno, L. (1985). A factorial experiment in teachers' written feedback on student homework: Changing teacher behaviour a little rather than a lot. *Journal of Educational Psychology, 77*(2), 162–173.

Elshout-Mohr, M. (1994). Feedback in self-instruction. *European Education, 26*(2), 58–73.

Even, R. & Tirosh, D. (1995). Subject-matter knowledge and the knowledge about students as sources of teacher presentations of the subject-matter. *Educational Studies in Mathematics, 29*(1), 1–20.

Fennema, E., Carpenter, T. P., Franke, M. L., Levi, L., Jacobs, V. R. & Empson, S. B. (1996). A longitudinal study of learning to use children's thinking in mathematics instruction. *Journal for Research in Mathematics Education, 27*(4), 403–434.

Fernandes, M. & Fontana, D. (1996). Changes in control beliefs in Portuguese primary school pupils as a consequence of the employment of self-assessment strategies. *British Journal of Educational Psychology, 66*(3), 301–313.

Flavell, J. H. (1976). Metacognitive aspects of problem solving. In L. B. Resnick (Ed.), *The nature of intelligence* (pp. 231–235). Hillsdale, NJ: Erlbaum.

Flynn, J. R. (2007). *What is intelligence?* Cambridge, England: Cambridge University Press.

Fontana, D. & Fernandes, M. (1994). Improvements in mathematics performance as a consequence of self-assessment in Portuguese primary school pupils. *British Journal of Educational Psychology, 64*(4), 407–417.

Foos, P. W., Mora, J. J. & Tkacz, S. (1994). Student study techniques and the generation effect. *Journal of Educational Psychology, 86*(4), 567–576.

Franke, M. L., Carpenter, T. P., Levi, L. & Fennema, E. (2001). Capturing teachers' generative change: A follow-up study of professional development in mathematics. *American Educational Research Journal, 38*(3), 653–689.

Fuchs, L. S. & Fuchs, D. (1986). Effects of systematic formative evaluation—a meta-analysis. *Exceptional Children, 53*(3), 199–208.

Garet, M. S., Cronen, S., Easton, M., Kurki, A., Ludwig, M., Jones, W. et al. (2008). *The impact of two professional development interventions on early reading instruction and achievement* (NCEE No. 2008–4030). Washington, DC: Institute of Education Sciences, National Center for Education Evaluation and Regional Assistance.

Garet, M. S., Wayne, A. J., Stancavage, F., Taylor, J., Walters, K., Song, M. et al. (2010). *Middle school mathematics professional development impact study: Findings after the first year of implementation* (NCEE No. 2010–4009). Washington, DC: Institute of Education Sciences, National Center for Education Evaluation and Regional Assistance.

Gipps, C. V. & Stobart, G. (1997). *Assessment: A teacher's guide to the issues* (3rd ed.). London: Hodder & Stoughton.

Gladwell, M. (2008a, December 15). Most likely to succeed. *New Yorker,* 36–42.

Gladwell, M. (2008b). *Outliers: The story of success.* New York: Little, Brown.

Goe, L. & Bridgeman, B. (2006). *Effects of Focus on Standards on academic performance.* Princeton, NJ: Educational Testing Service.

Goldin, C. & Katz, L. F. (2008). *The race between education and technology.* Cambridge, MA: Harvard University Press.

Good, T. L. & Grouws, D. A. (1975). *Process-product relationships in fourth grade mathematics classrooms* (Grant No. NEG-00-3-0123). Columbia: University of Missouri.

Goodgame, D. (2000, August 14). *The game of risk.* Accessed at www.time.com /time/magazine/article/0,9171,997709,00.html on October 20, 2010.

Goswami, U. (2006). Neuroscience and education: From research to practice? *Nature Reviews Neuroscience, 7*(5), 406–411.

Gray, E. M. & Tall, D. O. (1994). Duality, ambiguity and flexibility: A "proceptual" view of simple arithmetic. *Journal for Research in Mathematics Education, 25*(2), 116–140.

Hacker, D. J., Dunlosky, J. & Graesser, A. C. (Eds.). (1998). *Metacognition in educational theory and practice.* Mahwah, NJ: Lawrence Erlbaum Associates.

Hamre, B. K. & Pianta, R. C. (2005). Academic and social advantages for at-risk students placed in high quality first grade classrooms. *Child Development, 76*(5), 949–967.

Hanushek, E. A. (2010). Teacher deselection. In D. Goldhaber & J. Hannaway (Eds.), *Creating a new teaching profession* (pp. 165–180). Washington, DC: Urban Institute Press.

Hanushek, E. A. & Rivkin, S. G. (2006). Teacher quality. In E. A. Hanushek & F. Welsh (Eds.), *Handbook of the economics of education* (Vol. 2, pp. 1051–1078). Amsterdam: Elsevier.

Hanushek, E. A. & Woessmann, L. (2010). *The high cost of low educational performance: The long-run impact of improving PISA outcomes.* Paris: Organisation for Economic Co-operation and Development.

Harlen, W. & Deakin Crick, R. (2002). *A systematic review of the impact of summative assessment and tests on students' motivation for learning.* London: EPPI-Centre, Social Science Research Unit, Institute of Education. Accessed at http://eppi.ioe.ac.uk/cms/LinkClick.aspx?fileticket=rOyQ%2ff 4y3TI%3d on August 31, 2010.

Hart, K. M., Brown, M. L., Kerslake, D., Küchemann, D., & Ruddock, G. (1985). *Chelsea diagnostic mathematics tests.* Windsor, UK: NFER-Nelson.

Hattie, J. & Timperley, H. (2007). The power of feedback. *Review of Educational Research, 77*(1), 81–112.

Hayes, V. P. (2003). *Using pupil self-evaluation within the formative assessment paradigm as a pedagogical tool.* Unpublished doctoral dissertation, University of London.

Heid, M. K., Blume, G. W., Zbiek, R. M. & Edwards, B. S. (1999). Factors that influence teachers learning to do interviews to understand students' mathematical understandings. *Educational Studies in Mathematics, 37*(3), 223–249.

Hiebert, J., Gallimore, R., Garnier, H., Givvin, K. B., Hollingsworth, H., Jacobs, J. K. et al. (2003). *Teaching mathematics in seven countries: Results from the TIMSS 1999 video study* (NCES No. 2003–013). Washington, DC: National Center for Education Statistics.

Hill, H. C. & Ball, D. L. (2004). Learning mathematics for teaching: Results from California's mathematics professional development institutes. *Journal for Research in Mathematics Education, 35*(5), 330–351.

Hill, H. C., Rowan, B. & Ball, D. L. (2005). Effects of teachers' mathematical knowledge for teaching on student achievement. *American Educational Research Journal, 42*(2), 371–406.

Hill, P. T., Angel, L. & Christensen, J. (2006). Charter school achievement studies. *Education Finance and Policy, 1*(1), 139–150.

Hines, T. (1987). Left brain/right brain mythology and implications for management and training. *Academy of Management Review, 12*(4), 600–606.

Hodgen, J., & Wiliam, D. (2006). *Mathematics inside the black box: Assessment for learning in the mathematics classroom.* London: NFER-Nelson.

Howard-Jones, P. (2009). *Neuroscience and education: Issues and opportunities.* London: Institute of Education, University of London.

Howson, J. (2010, May 21). Premium pay for the very few. *Times Educational Supplement,* pp. 24–25.

Hoxby, C. & Rockoff, J. E. (2004). *The impact of charter schools on student achievement.* Cambridge, MA: Harvard University.

Ingersoll, R. M. (Ed.). (2007). *A comparative study of teacher preparation and qualifications in six nations.* Philadelphia: Consortium for Policy Research in Education.

Jagger, C., Matthews, R., Melzer, D., Matthews, F., Brayne, C. & MRC Cognitive Function and Ageing Study. (2007). Educational differences in the dynamics of disability incidence, recovery and mortality: Findings from the MRC Cognitive Function and Ageing Study (MRC CFAS). *International Journal of Epidemiology, 36,* 358–365.

James, M. (1992). *Assessment for learning.* Paper presented at the annual conference of the Association for Supervision and Curriculum Development, New Orleans, LA.

Jones, J. & Wiliam, D. (2007). *Modern foreign languages inside the black box: Assessment for learning in the modern foreign languages classroom.* London: Granada.

Jordan, M. (2009). Acceptance speech to the National Basketball Association's Hall of Fame. Accessed at www.nba.com/video/channels/hall_of_fame/2009 /09/11/nba_20090911_hof_jordan_speech.nba/ on August 16, 2010.

Kahl, S. (2005). Where in the world are formative tests? Right under your nose! *Education Week, 25*(4), 11.

Karmiloff-Smith, A., & Inhelder, B. (1974/1975). If you want to get ahead, get a theory. *Cognition, 3*(3), 195–212.

Keddie, N. (1971). Classroom knowledge. In M. F. D. Young (Ed.), *Knowledge and control.* London: Collier-Macmillan.

Kling, A. S., & Schulz, N. (2009). *From poverty to prosperity: Intangible assets, hidden liabilities and the lasting triumph over scarcity.* New York: Encounter Books.

Kluger, A. N., & DeNisi, A. (1996). The effects of feedback interventions on performance: A historical review, a meta-analysis, and a preliminary feedback intervention theory. *Psychological Bulletin, 119*(2), 254–284.

Kohn, A. (1994). Grading: The issue is not how but why. *Educational Leadership, 52*(2), 38–41.

Kohn, A. (2006). The trouble with rubrics. *English Journal, 95*(4), 12–15.

Köller, O. (2005). Formative assessment in classrooms: A review of the empirical German literature. In J. Looney (Ed.), *Formative assessment: Improving learning in secondary classrooms* (pp. 265–279). Paris: Organisation for Economic Co-operation and Development.

Leahy, S., Lyon, C., Thompson, M., & Wiliam, D. (2005). Classroom assessment: Minute-by-minute and day-by-day. *Educational Leadership, 63*(3), 18–24.

Leahy, S., & Wiliam, D. (2009). *Embedding assessment for learning—a professional development pack*. London: Specialist Schools and Academies Trust.

Leigh, A. (2010). Estimating teacher effectiveness from two-year changes in students' test scores. *Economics of Education Review, 29*(3), 480–488.

Lemov, D. (2010). *Teach like a champion: 49 techniques that put students on the path to college*. San Francisco: Jossey-Bass.

Levin, H. M., Belfield, C., Muennig, P., & Rouse, C. (2007). *The costs and benefits of an excellent education for all of America's children*. New York: Teachers College Press.

Lewis, C. C. (2002). *Lesson study: A handbook of teacher-led instructional change*. Philadelphia: Research for Better Schools.

Linnenbrink, E. A. (2005). The dilemma of performance-approach goals: The use of multiple goal contexts to promote students' motivation and learning. *Journal of Educational Psychology, 97*(2), 197–213.

Lleras-Muney, A. (2005). The relationship between education and adult mortality in the United States. *Review of Economic Studies, 72*(1), 189–221.

Lodico, M. G., Ghatala, E. S., Levin, J. R., Pressley, M., & Bell, J. A. (1983). The effects of strategy-monitoring training on children's selection of effective memory strategies. *Journal of Experimental Child Psychology, 35*(2), 263–277.

Looney, J. (Ed.). (2005). *Formative assessment: Improving learning in secondary classrooms*. Paris: Organisation for Economic Cooperation and Development.

Ma, L. (1999). *Knowing and teaching elementary mathematics: Teachers' understanding of fundamental mathematics in China and the United States*. Mahwah, NJ: Erlbaum.

Machin, S. & McNally, S. (2009, May). *The three Rs: What scope is there for literacy and numeracy policies to raise pupil achievement?* Paper presented at the Beyond the Resource Constraint: Alternative Ways to Improve Schooling seminar of the Research Institute for Industrial Economics, London, England.

Machin, S. & Wilson, J. (2009). Academy schools and pupil performance. *CentrePiece, 14*(1), 6–7.

Maher, J. & Wiliam, D. (2007, April). *Keeping learning on track in new teacher induction*. Paper presented at the annual conference of the American Educational Research Association, Chicago, IL.

Mangan, J., Pugh, G. & Gray, J. (2007, September). *Examination performance and school expenditure in English secondary schools in a dynamic setting*. Paper presented at the annual conference of the British Educational Research Association, London, England.

Mehan, H. (1979). *Learning lessons: Social organization in the classroom.* Cambridge, MA: Harvard University Press.

Mercer, N., Dawes, L., Wegerif, R. & Sams, C. (2004). Reasoning as a scientist: Ways of helping children to use language to learn science. *British Educational Research Journal, 30*(3), 359–377.

Mirabile, M. P. (2005). Intelligence and football: Testing for differentials in collegiate quarterback passing performance and NFL compensation. *The Sport Journal, 8*(2). Accessed at www.thesportjournal.org/article/intelligence-and-football -testing-differentials-collegiate-quarterback-passing-performance-a on August 21, 2010.

Miron, G. & Urschel, J. L. (2010). *Equal or fair? A study of revenues and expenditures in American charter schools.* Boulder, CO: Education and the Public Interest Center.

Morgan, D. (1965). *Guitar: The book that teaches you everything you need to know about playing the guitar.* London: Corgi.

Moss, G., Jewitt, C., Levačić, R., Armstrong, V., Cardini, A. & Castle, F. (2007). *The interactive whiteboards, pedagogy and pupil performance evaluation: An evaluation of the Schools Whiteboard Expansion (SWE) project: London challenge* (Research Report No. RR816). London: Department for Education and Skills.

National Assessment of Educational Progress. (2005). NAEP questions tool. Accessed at http://nces.ed.gov/nationsreportcard/itmrlsx/search.aspx ?subject=mathematics on December 1, 2005.

Natriello, G. (1987). The impact of evaluation processes on students. *Educational Psychologist, 22*(2), 155–175.

Neisser, U. (Ed.). (1998). *The rising curve: Long-term gains in IQ and related measures.* Washington, DC: American Psychological Association.

Nye, B. A., Konstantopoulos, S. & Hedges, L. V. (2004). How large are teacher effects? *Educational Evaluation and Policy Analysis, 26*(3), 237–257.

Nyquist, J. B. (2003). *The benefits of reconstruing feedback as a larger system of formative assessment: A meta-analysis.* Unpublished master's thesis, Vanderbilt University.

Organisation for Economic Co-operation and Development. (2010). *Education at a glance.* Paris: Author.

Papert, S. A. (1998, June 2). *Child power: Keys to the new learning of the digital century.* Paper presented at the 11th Colin Cherry Memorial Lecture on Communication, London, England.

Patel, R., Kelly, S., Amadeo, C., Gracey, S. & Meyer, B. (2009). *Beyond Leitch: Skills policy for the upturn.* London: Learning and Skills Network.

Pickeral, R. (2009, September 9). Jordan the competitor. *Charlotte Observer,* C1.

Pirsig, R. M. (1991). *Lila: An inquiry into morals.* New York: Bantam Books.

Polanyi, M. (1958). *Personal knowledge.* Chicago: University of Chicago Press.

Polanyi, M. (1966). *The tacit dimension.* New York: Doubleday.

Polya, G. (1945). *How to solve it: A new aspect of mathematical method.* Princeton, NJ: Princeton University Press.

Popham, W. J. (2006). Phony formative assessments: Buyer beware! *Educational Leadership,* 64(3), 86–87.

Programme for International Student Assessment. (2007). *PISA 2006: Science competences for tomorrow's world* (Vol. 1). Paris: Organisation for Economic Co-operation and Development.

Rampey, B. D., Dion, G. S. & Donahue, P. L. (2009). *NAEP 2008: Trends in academic progress* (Vol. NCES 2009–479). Washington, DC: U.S. Department of Education.

Raven, J. (1960). *Guide to the standard progressive matrices: Sets A, B, C and D.* London: Lewis.

Relearning by Design. (2000). *What is a rubric?* Accessed at www.pepartnership .org/media/12821/Rubrics.pdf? on March 9, 2011.

Ritter, S., Anderson, J. R., Koedinger, K. R. & Corbett, A. (2007). Cognitive tutor: Applied research in mathematics education. *Psychonomic Bulletin & Review, 14*(2), 249–255.

Rivkin, S. G., Hanushek, E. A. & Kain, J. F. (2005). Teachers, schools and academic achievement. *Econometrica, 73*(2), 417–458.

Rockoff, J. E. (2004). The impact of individual teachers on student achievement: Evidence from panel data. *American Economic Review, 94*(2), 247–252.

Rowan, B., Harrison, D. M. & Hayes, A. (2004). Using instructional logs to study mathematics curriculum and teaching in the early grades. *Elementary School Journal, 105,* 103–127.

Rowe, M. B. (1974). Wait time and rewards as instructional variables: Their influence on language, learning and fate control. *Journal of Research in Science Teaching, 11,* 81–94.

Ryan, R. M. & Deci, E. L. (2000). Intrinsic and extrinsic motivations: Classic definitions and new directions. *Contemporary Educational Psychology, 25,* 54–67.

Ryle, G. (1949). *The concept of mind*. London: Hutchinson.

Sadler, D. R. (1989). Formative assessment and the design of instructional systems. *Instructional Science, 18*, 119–144.

Sanders, W. L. & Rivers, J. C. (1996). *Cumulative and residual effects of teachers on future student academic achievement*. Knoxville, TN: University of Tennessee Value-Added Research and Assessment Center. Accessed at www.heartland.org/custom/semod_policybot/pdf/3048.pdf on August 21, 2010.

Saphier, J. (2005). Masters of motivation. In R. DuFour, R. Eaker, & R. DuFour (Eds.), *On common ground: The power of professional learning communities* (pp. 85–113). Bloomington, IN: Solution Tree Press (formerly National Educational Service).

Schacter, J. (2000). Does individual tutoring produce optimal learning? *American Educational Research Journal, 37*(3), 801–829.

Schoenfeld, A. H. (1989). Explorations of students' mathematical beliefs and behavior. *Journal for Research in Mathematics Education, 20*(4), 338–355.

Schunk, D. H. (1991). Self-efficacy and academic motivation. *Educational Psychologist, 26*, 207–231.

Schwartz, B. (2003). *The paradox of choice: Why more is less*. New York: Ecco.

Scriven, M. (1967). The methodology of evaluation. In R. W. Tyler, R. M. Gagné, & M. Scriven (Eds.), *Perspectives of curriculum evaluation* (Vol. 1, pp. 39–83). Chicago: RAND.

Serwer, A. (2010, June 5). John Wooden's best coaching tip: Listen [Web log post]. Accessed at http://money.cnn.com/2010/06/05/news/newsmakers/john _wooden_obituary_fortune.fortune/index.htm on January 1, 2011.

Shepard, L. A. (2008). Formative assessment: Caveat emptor. In C. A. Dwyer (Ed.), *The future of assessment: Shaping teaching and learning* (pp. 279–303). Mahwah, NJ: Erlbaum.

Shepard, L. A., Hammerness, K., Darling-Hammond, L., Rust, F., Snowden, J. B., Gordon, E. et al. (2007). Assessment. In L. Darling-Hammond & J. Bransford (Eds.), *Preparing teachers for a changing world: What teachers should learn and be able to do* (pp. 275–326). Melbourne, Victoria: Hawker Brownlow Education.

Shute, V. J. (2008). Focus on formative feedback. *Review of Educational Research, 78*(1), 153–189.

Simmons, M. & Cope, P. (1993). Angle and rotation: Effects of differing types of feedback on the quality of response. *Educational Studies in Mathematics,*

24(2), 163–176.

Slater, H., Davies, N. & Burgess, S. (2008). *Do teachers matter? Measuring the variation in teacher effectiveness in England* (Working Paper No. 09/212). Bristol, England: Bristol Institute of Public Affairs.

Slavin, R. E. (1995). *Cooperative learning: Theory, research and practice* (2nd ed.). Boston: Allyn & Bacon.

Slavin, R. E., Hurley, E. A. & Chamberlain, A. M. (2003). Cooperative learning and achievement. In W. M. Reynolds & G. J. Miller (Eds.), *Handbook of psychology: Vol. 7. Educational psychology* (pp. 177–198). Hoboken, NJ: Wiley.

Slavin, R. E. & Lake, C. (2008). Effective programs in elementary mathematics: A best-evidence synthesis. *Review of Research in Education, 78*(3), 427–515.

Slavin, R. E., Lake, C., Chambers, B., Cheung, A. & Davis, S. (2009). Effective reading programs for the elementary grades: A best-evidence synthesis. *Review of Research in Education, 79*(4), 1391–1466.

Slavin, R. E., Lake, C. & Groff, C. (2009). Effective programs in middle and high school mathematics: A best-evidence synthesis. *Review of Research in Education, 79*(3), 839–911.

Smith, I. (2008). *Sharing learning outcomes*. Cambridge, England: Cambridge Education.

Smithers, A. & Robinson, P. (2009). *Specialist science schools*. Buckingham, UK: University of Buckingham Centre for Education and Employment Research.

Spradbery, J. (1976). Conservative pupils? Pupil resistance to curriculum innovation in mathematics. In M. F. D. Young & G. Whitty (Eds.), *Explorations into the politics of school knowledge* (pp. 236–243). Driffield, England: Nafferton.

Springer, L., Stanne, M. E. & Donovan, S. S. (1999). Effects of small-group learning on undergraduates in science, mathematics, engineering and technology: A meta-analysis. *Review of Educational Research, 69*(1), 21–51.

Springer, M. G., Ballou, D., Hamilton, L., Le, V.-N., Lockwood, J. R., McCaffrey, D. et al. (2010). *Teacher pay for performance: Experimental evidence from the project on incentives in teaching*. Nashville, TN: National Center on Performance Incentives.

Stanovich, K. E. (1986). Matthew effects in reading: Some consequences of individual differences in the acquisition of literacy. *Reading Research Quarterly, 21*(4), 360–407.

Stevens, R. J. & Slavin, R. E. (1995). Effects of a cooperative learning approach in reading and writing on academically handicapped and nonhandicapped students. *Elementary School Journal, 95*(3), 241–262.

Stiggins, R. J. (2001). *Student-involved classroom assessment* (3rd ed.). Upper Saddle River, NJ: Prentice Hall.

Stiggins, R. J. (2002). Assessment crisis: The absence of assessment FOR learning. *Phi Delta Kappan, 83*(10), 758–765.

Stiggins, R. J. (2005). From formative assessment to assessment FOR learning: A path to success in standards-based schools. *Phi Delta Kappan, 87*(4), 324–328.

Stiggins, R. J. & Chappuis, J. (2006). What a difference a word makes: Assessment FOR learning rather than assessment OF learning helps students succeed. *Journal of Staff Development, 27*(1), 10–15.

Sutton, R. (1995). *Assessment for learning.* Salford, England: RS Publications.

Thrupp, M. (1999). *Schools making a difference: Let's be realistic!* Buckingham, England: Open University Press.

Tobin, K. (1987). The role of wait time in higher cognitive level learning. *Review of Educational Research, 57*(1), 69–95.

Torrance, E. P. (1962). *Guiding creative talent.* Englewood Cliffs, NJ: Prentice Hall.

United Nations Statistics Division. (2010). *National accounts main aggregates database.* Accessed at http://unstats.un.org/unsd/snaama/dnlList.asp on November 1, 2010.

Vasquez Heilig, J. & Jez, S. J. (2010). *Teach for America: A review of the evidence.* Tempe: Arizona State University Education Policy Research Unit.

Vinner, S. (1997). From intuition to inhibition—mathematics, education and other endangered species. In E. Pehkonen (Ed.), *Proceedings of the 21st conference of the International Group for the Psychology of Mathematics Education* (Vol. 1, pp. 63–78). Lahti, Finland: University of Helsinki Lahti Research and Training Centre.

Waugh, E. (2001). *Decline and fall.* London: Penguin.

Webb, N. M. (1991). Task-related verbal interaction and mathematics learning in small groups. *Journal for Research in Mathematics Education, 22*(5), 366–389.

Weisberg, D. S., Keil, F. C., Goodstein, J., Rawson, E. & Gray, J. R. (2008). The seductive allure of neuroscience explanations. *Journal of Cognitive Neuroscience, 20*(3), 470–477.

Weiss, I. R., Pasley, J. D., Smith, P. S., Banilower, E. R. & Heck, D. J. (2003). *Looking inside the classroom: A study of K-12 mathematics and science education in the United States.* Chapel Hill, NC: Horizon Research.

Welch, J. & Welch, S. (2005). *Winning.* New York: Harper Business.

White, B. Y. & Frederiksen, J. R. (1998). Inquiry, modeling, and metacognition: Making science accessible to all students. *Cognition and Instruction, 16*(1), 3–118.

White, M. A. (1971). The view from the student's desk. In M. L. Silberman (Ed.), *The experience of schooling* (pp. 337–345). New York: Holt, Rinehart and Winston.

Wigfield, A., Eccles, J. S. & Rodriguez, D. (1998). The development of children's motivation in school contexts. In P. D. Pearson & A. Iran-Nejad (Eds.), *Review of research in education* (Vol. 23, pp. 73–118). Washington, DC: American Educational Research Association.

Wiggins, G. & McTighe, J. (2000, 2005). *Understanding by design.* Melbourne, Victoria: Hawker Brownlow Education.

Wiliam, D. (1999). Formative assessment in mathematics. Part 1: Rich questioning. *Equals: Mathematics and Special Educational Needs, 5*(2), 15–18.

Wiliam, D. (2005, April). *Measuring "intelligence": What can we learn and how can we move forward?* Paper presented at the annual meeting of the American Educational Research Association, Montreal, Quebec, Canada.

Wiliam, D. (2006). Assessment: Learning communities can use it to engineer a bridge connecting teaching and learning. *Journal of Staff Development, 27*(1), 16–20.

Wiliam, D. (2007a). Content *then* process: Teacher learning communities in the service of formative assessment. In D. B. Reeves (Ed.), *Ahead of the curve: The power of assessment to transform teaching and learning* (pp. 183–204). Bloomington, IN: Solution Tree Press.

Wiliam, D. (2007b). Keeping learning on track: Classroom assessment and the regulation of learning. In F. K. Lester, Jr. (Ed.), *Second handbook of mathematics teaching and learning* (pp. 1053–1098). Greenwich, CT: Information Age.

Wiliam, D. (2009). An integrative summary of the research literature and implications for a new theory of formative assessment. In H. L. Andrade & G. J. Cizek (Eds.), *Handbook of formative assessment.* New York: Taylor & Francis.

Wiliam, D., & Black, P. J. (1996). Meanings and consequences: A basis for distinguishing formative and summative functions of assessment? *British Educational Research Journal, 22*(5), 537–548.

Wiliam, D., Lee, C., Harrison, C. & Black, P. J. (2004). Teachers developing assessment for learning: Impact on student achievement. *Assessment in*

Education: Principles, Policy and Practice, 11(1), 49–65.

Wiliam, D. & Lester, F. K., Jr. (2008). On the purpose of mathematics education research: Making productive contributions to policy and practice. In L. D. English (Ed.), *Handbook of international research in mathematics education* (2nd ed., pp. 32–48). New York: Routledge.

Wiliam, D. & Thompson, M. (2008). Integrating assessment with instruction: What will it take to make it work? In C. A. Dwyer (Ed.), *The future of assessment: Shaping teaching and learning* (pp. 53–82). Mahwah, NJ: Erlbaum.

Williamson, M. (1992). *A return to love.* New York: HarperCollins.

Wilson, M. & Draney, K. (2004). Some links between large-scale and classroom assessments: The case of the BEAR Assessment System. In M. Wilson (Ed.), *Towards coherence between classroom assessment and accountability: The 103rd yearbook of the National Society for the Study of Education, part 2* (pp. 132–154). Chicago: University of Chicago Press.

Winne, P. H. (1996). A metacognitive view of individual differences in self-regulated learning. *Learning and Individual Differences, 8,* 327–353.

Wolff, H. (Writer), & Jackson, M. (Director). (1983). The future is further away than you think [Television series episode]. In M. Jackson (Producer), *Q.E.D.* England: British Broadcasting Company.

Wylie, E. C. & Wiliam, D. (2006, April). *Diagnostic questions: Is there value in just one?* Paper presented at the annual meeting of the National Council on Measurement in Education, San Francisco, CA.

Yeh, S. S. (2006). *Raising student achievement through rapid assessment and test reform.* New York: Teachers College Press.

Yeh, S. S. (2009). The cost-effectiveness of NBPTS teacher certification. *Evaluation Review, 34*(3), 220–241.

Index